MW01697497

EARTHROAMER

By

Donny Dust

An Earthroamer is a person who ventures out into the backcountry, forests and natural world with no real plan, no goals and simply lives. Curiosity guides an Earthroamer from place to place. Curiosity lets the Earthroamer see and experience new places and experiences while relying on the most important survival and thrival skill of all: creativity. The hope is to walk into the wilds of the world with nothing and walk out with everything.

Special thanks to my friend and editor Sara Stibitz.

My appreciation, gratitude and respect for you is endless

You made this book come to life!

Table of Contents

Contents

Let curiosity guide you.

Introduction

In the Beginning

"Treat the earth well: it was not given to you by your parents, it was loaned to you by your children. We do not inherit the Earth from our Ancestors, we borrow it from our Children."

Unknown First Nations Source

For nearly thirty years I have been an Earthroamer, but for at least twenty of those years I had no idea what an Earthroamer was or even did. The word came to me eleven years ago while walking from the Salton Sea in Southern California to Twentynine Palms, California. I had stopped for the first night after walking what I thought was about seventeen miles that day, my first day of what I thought was a seventy-two-mile route.

That first day was hot with little to no reprieve from the sun. The rocky, sandy mountains I walked through unsystematically were barren in many spots and vacant of visible life, while other areas were covered in low scrub sage, cholla cactus and rabbitbrush. From the tracks and trails left by invisible desert creatures, I could see life did exist in this harsh and life-threatening environment, but a life that was highly adaptive and able. I needed to adapt once again to survive.

No natural water sources existed in the area I was walking through from what I could see. Only deep, underground aquifers and seasonal rains offered life to continue in this region of the

US. I am sure small springs existed, but that is a secret kept by the desert. Days before I departed on this Earthroam I hiked from my endpoint to a general midpoint of my semi-planned route and cached about three gallons of water under a large rock. This would serve as my only opportunity to refill on water.

The day continued with intense heat. I walked miles through long stretches of rocky open areas offering no shade and endless amounts of direct sun. Thirst was somewhat of an enemy and it served as a constant reminder to refill my body of precious water often or possibly face death. A small sliver of shade cast by a tough and tall desert plant was the only opportunity to find relief from the intensity overhead. The isolation and exposure I encountered is something that few people will intentionally endure; however, I found an aspect of peace and connection to the surrounding landscape. I knew that eventually she – nature, that is – would provide what I needed. She had done so many times before, but until that moment came, I kept walking.

When night finally started to fall, a sense of relief from the intense sun took over my body, but only for a short time. Temperatures quickly drop in the desert once the sun settles in the West for the night. This causes a once sunbaked landscape to turn nearly polar-like in a short time after the sun is completely gone from sight. Having lived in many deserts this was to be expected. Shelter from the cold, wind, and creatures was a must.

My shelter for the night was a small rock overhang that faced West and was ideal for one night of sleep. The rock overhang conveniently caught the last traces of sunlight before the sun completely disappeared and night fully took over. This made it ideal to sleep in as it acted like a thermal heater for a few hours after sunset. However, before I could wrap myself up in a wool blanket and tuck in for the night, I needed to clear my luxurious arrangements of any snakes, spiders, and scorpions because they were attracted to that overhang for all the same reasons that I was.

As I laid under my overhang, looking at the last traces of sunlight and counting the first evening stars, I had a realization. An idea struck me that went against every principle and fundamental rule of remote backcountry travel that had ever existed. An idea that would make any outdoorsmen, adventurer, survival instructor, hunter, teacher, police officer, military member, backpacker, skier, grandparent, parent, anyone cringe. I had no plan for this backcountry, remote, solo adventure. No real plan at all. Nothing!

I joined the United States Marine Corps in 1999 and having a plan was the one thing the Marines did well. There was a plan for everything, as there should be. The military exists to support and defend America and fight in her wars and the Marines are the warfighters. Even when not fighting or preparing for combat, our daily routines were planned out: Reville 0530; 0600 PT Formation; PT 0615-0830; Shit, shower, shave 0830-0900; Daily Duties 0900-1130; Midday chow 1130-1300; Daily Duties 1300-1600; aternoon formation 1600-1630, and that is when you received the plan for the next day. Effective? Yes!

We had a plan to eat, a plan to shit, a plan to travel and a plan for combat. Hell, we had a saying that, *the first thing that dies in combat is the plan*. So, we had secondary and tertiary plans in case the primary plan failed. We worked into our planning meetings to have new planning meetings if the first plan in the original planning meeting was not executed because of a different external plan changing, thus resulting in our plan shifting to the secondary plan. See where I'm going with this? Planning was a constant.

For this particular trip, I had a general idea to start at the Salton Sea, refill water at my cached water point, and finish in Twentynine Palms. That was it. Nothing more. My first day was spent walking aimlessly through valleys and washes, letting curiosity guide me. I don't even know if I walked seventeen miles that first day. It felt like seventeen miles, so it must have been seventeen miles. Hell, I didn't even know where I was. I knew where I was at a macro level, but I couldn't find it on a map because I didn't bring one. I had no compass, no flashlight, no tent, no phone, no sunscreen, no stove, no whistle, basically nothing. And I did not care. I was ok not having a plan. I was ok not having pounds of gear, or waypoints to mark my progress along a route. I was fine not having an exact location of where I slept that night. I was fine not having food and comfort items. I was perfectly fine in all and every way. I was ok!

Keep in mind that my lack of planning did not grow from negligence, carelessness, or lack of experience. It did not come from being spiteful of the military because there was a plan for a plan. No, it was the complete opposite, which will become clear later in the book.

Wrapped in my wool blanket and the complete darkness, I drifted back to the start of the day, right after my wife dropped me off. I began to think about how I started in one spot and how I eventually found this rock overhang. I retraced my route in my mind, replaying each valley, dry wash, and rocky hill-climb in my mind. I came to the assumption that my day was controlled and directed by my own curiosity.

I had never consciously thought of this; curiosity controlling my actions and movements. I recalled about an hour or two into my trek that I had come across some coyote tracks and followed them over a series of hills that lead me to a few rusted out abandoned cars that looked like they belonged in a 1920's mobster movie. From Al Capone's getaway car, I saw what I thought was a cave on a distant mountain face, but on closer inspection it turned out to be an old mine. From the mine, I smelled something rotting and followed my nose; from the rotting coyote I saw a rock formation that looked like a castle tower and thought it might be an awesome vantage point to scout surrounding areas; after taking over the castle I could clearly see a long deep wash in the distance and wanted to see what was around the bend; nothing was around the bend in the wash except more wash, but at the bend I heard a strange scream or screech and followed the sound; I never found its owner, but I discovered some West- facing rock ledges and decided to make one my home for the night. Boom… seventeen miles, maybe twenty – I couldn't tell you either way – crossed in curiosity.

Curiosity pulled me from one location to the other. I roamed about without a plan. No direction. No requirements. I roamed freely and without concern for where I was going. I knew I was going somewhere, but where that somewhere was, I didn't know. It turns out that on that day, I was going to a small rock overhang that was my home for the night – where the idea of Earthroaming would first come to me.

Chapter 1

Earthroam Defined

"In every walk with nature one receives far more than he seeks."

John Muir

Earthroaming is moving about the environment with no real plan, letting only curiosity guide you from place to place. Earthroaming is a style and method of adventuring or exploring where the "Earthroamer" moves about an area unsystematically, in a natural or manmade environment, with no real plan in mind. The idea is to be led by curiosity until you find a reason to stop, return home, or call it a day. It is entirely up to you! Earthroaming does not require that you have no destination in mind, a flexible course of action, or even an end date, but the concept is to let curiosity guide you along your Earthroam.

This book is designed to lay out the concept of Earthroaming for you. But first, let me tell you what Earthroaming isn't. It is not a super-special, ultra-elite, cost-you-a-fortune-to-join club. It is not a piece of gear. It is not a set of strict rules that a person must live by or you will be kicked out of the club. In all honesty you can make this concept work however it benefits you and your pattern of life. Earthroaming *is* an idea and an approach to exploring the backcountry, the woods, deserts, jungles, mountains, anywhere a person might venture in a new way. Simply put, the definition of Earthroaming can be found in its name.

1. ***Earth:*** the planet on which we live; the world, substance of land; soil.

2. ***Roam**:* walk aimlessly, move about a large area unsystematically, or simply move about.

Combined together you have *walk aimlessly over the earth or move about a large area of earth unsystematically, or simply move about the earth.* Pretty simple when you think about it. However, I must add to two crucial elements to obtaining the full benefits of an Earthroam: curiosity and a lack of specific plans.

There are a couple of reasons I think this idea is important today, and these reasons form the basis of why I'm sharing it with you. First, to truly be free and thrive in the backcountry or the wilds of the world, you must let go of everything and fully immerse oneself in the natural world. A real connection to the natural world can be obtained through Earthroaming. A mental, physical, emotional and primal connection are just a few of the healthy outcomes one can obtain from an Earthroam. We are missing a connection, a feeling of comfort in the natural world. When we domesticated ourselves and desired that what was labeled as necessary, we lost our innate relationship to the natural world. Earthroaming brings us back to the land and firmly plants us in a state of well being.

Second, Earthroaming presents a real-life scenario, event, or practical environment for many survivalists, bushcrafters, and primitive skills practitioners to employ their skills. Consider Earthroaming to be a true test of a person's ability to recall knowledge and apply their skills. Earthroaming is a real experience of living remotely and applying life-sustaining knowledge, skills, and abilities.

Lastly, Earthroaming offers a different approach to outdoor activities and experiences by promoting creativity instead of overlooking it. You will hear me say it many times: creativity is the number one survival skill. Hell, creativity is one of the most important life skills in general. Nothing in this world would exist without it. We would not exist without it. Everything we come across in some way, shape or form is a result of the creative process. Earthroaming does not just feed the spark of creativity. Earthroaming is the fuel for the creative mind to light a blaze with possibilities.

Chapter 2

Core Concepts of Earthroaming

"Earth and sky, woods and fields, lakes and rivers, the mountain and the sea, are excellent schoolmasters, and teach us more than we can ever learn from books."

John Lubbock

So, you can better understand Earthroaming, I want to provide a few core concepts that will enable you to fully embrace becoming an Earthroamer. Again, these concepts are just some best practices and consideration points to fully enable an adventurous and meaningful Earthroam.

Allow Your *Curiosity to Lead.*

Earthroaming is led by your curiosity. It's simple, really. When you fully immerse yourself in the environment you are earthroaming in, just be curious. If a distant mountain, or a soaring eagle, or a running stream pulls you in one direction over another, just go with it. If you see *something* in the distance and want to discover what it is, just go with it. Curiosity is the best guide in life. Curiosity has led us to new lands, even to the moon. Curiosity is ingrained in all of us and we must not forget it.

It's far too easy and common for people to stick to the path. They put their head down and walk, rarely looking up to see what the natural world has to offer. They lose focus and fixate on the goal and that's it. People become hyper-focused on the end location and forget to take in the world around them. This eliminates their connection to the land and stifles curiosity.

I heard of a man who did the Colorado Trail in ten days. The Colorado trail is a trail that extends between Denver and Durango, Colorado. It's about five hundred miles long and this gentleman did it in ten days. That's about fifty miles a day. His accomplishment was a great success and show of endurance without a doubt, but why are we in such a hurry? Why are we trying to set a record, when the biggest trophies are all around us in the natural world? I can guarantee you that, more than once, this gentleman saw something that sparked his curiosity and he did not follow it. He was probably worried about meeting his goal. His thoughts were probably *I have to hit my goal...got to get to fifty... what's that... that looks cool... I should check that out... wait, I need to get my fifty miles in... stay focused... that's your goal.* Again, good on him for achieving what he wanted, but with Earthroaming the idea is to spend as much time in the wilds of the world as possible while letting curiosity guide you.

Long before I coined the term Earthroaming, my natural curiosity could be sparked by a sound, a distant shape, a fleeing animal, a stream, a light, a smell, or *gut feeling could* lead me to some amazing places. I know we have all done this before. Something catches our interest and we follow that curiosity. It feels good. It feels natural. I like to think of this natural feeling as an *innate curiosity* that has been handed down generation after generation. Our early ancestors were always moving from place to place, following herds, weather or even better, their innate curiosity of the land.

Know More and Carry Less.

The saying, *Know More and Carry Less,* is a popular saying among many outdoorsman and adventurers and has been a cornerstone of my approach to the outdoors for some time. I can carry far more in my brain than I can carry on my back. Knowing more and carrying less not only forces the Earthroamer to be well versed in survival skills, thrival skills and all manner of outdoor skills, but creates a better, more self-reliant and confident person.

I remember years and years ago I was defeated, flat out broke and fed up with all the *stuff* I had that was the "required" gear for a "true outdoor experience." What *stuff* you ask? All the overpriced, weigh-you-down, must-have bullshit that so many people fall prey to these days. Back then I had it all and at that time I believed I needed it, all of it. Packs, sleeping bags, stoves, water filtration systems, cookware, sleeping pads, tents, knives, headlamps, compression bags – the list could go on for several pages. I gave it all away. I decided that this stuff was taking away from my experiences and I no longer needed it. I had the knowledge and the skills, which did not require a $500.00 backpack or a $250.00 water filtration system.

I'm not saying that I don't bring the appropriate safety gear where needed, like with rock climbing. I am not saying that when you go backcountry skiing you should not have skis, helmet, avalanche rig, goggles and appropriate gear to battle the elements. What I am saying is that every situation is different and will require different types of stuff however, on an Earthroam, knowing more and carrying less means knowledge and skills are far more valuable when compared to unnecessary stuff.

Don't get me wrong, knowing more and carrying less is something that requires years of learning and education. It is something that cannot be learned overnight or picked up in a weekend survival training session, but it can be a concept to work from, a starting point, if you will. A point where you can say, I must be knowledgeable in a subject matter and I must be able to perform the skills associated with the knowledge set. This is called a pulse check. It is easy to know something but requires more effort and personal dedication to be able to routinely and accurately perform the associated tasks. I was only able to purge myself of the stuff because I was skilled in survival and thrival skills. At that time, I *knew more and carried more,* but eventually got rid of it all, truly became free, and now *know more and carry less.*

Have *No Real Plan.*

Not having a plan is hard for many people to fathom, but a true Earthroam lacks any type of real plan. Keep in mind that these are my concepts and if you need a few guiding plans to complete your Earthroam, have at it. I will never be the person who tells you that you are doing wrong because you are not doing it my way. You do you!

Keep it simple; the best way to have a creative, meaningful, connection filled Earthroam is to drop the plan. Clearly, there is a difference in planning for a snowshoeing adventure with my kids when compared to an Earthroam I conduct on my own or even with a friend or two. Different outdoor adventures require different degrees of planning.

In March of 2018 my kids and I embarked on a 24-hour backcountry trip in Southern Utah, walking from Boulder Utah to Escalante, Utah. It was a quick 20+ mile route known as the Mail Trail that would wind us through some of the most beautiful country Mother Nature has to offer. We followed a set of poorly placed cairns along the way, and my then-11-year-old son supplemented this ancient route by navigating using terrain association on an inaccurate topographic map. Everyone had one sleeping bag, a change of clothes, a few snacks, and two one-liter bottles of water. I carried all the same gear along with a metal pot to boil water in, a small first aid kit, and some extra clothes.

At every cliff edge, canyon bend and steep rock face, Mother Nature presented a new set of experiences for all of us. Along our route we ascended steep canyon walls, carefully meandered along cliff edges, walked through sun baked plateaus, played in streams, meticulously scrambled down steep canyon faces and rested in the shade of ancient Juniper Trees until we eventually reached a canyon that could be our home for the night. When we finally descended into our new canyon home, we collected wild edibles, drank from springs, built a fire under a high canyon overhang, and slept under the stars.

This adventure was epic in many ways. We had a small plan; start in Boulder Utah, end in Escalante, Utah, stop for one night, pack the bare essentials, follow the cairns and have fun. Down and dirty, really! Now, if this was an Earthroam for me, it might sound like this; start in Boulder, Utah, walk southwest until you come to Escalante, Utah; or start in Boulder Utah and walk until you are finished. Case by case, environment to environment, or person to person; every Earthroam for me is different.

Not having a plan can be scary, but please don't think that an overall concept or course of action is not of value. Nothing is wrong with informing someone of your intent. Actually, that is a great practice that everyone needs to do – inform others. Something like; start at this trailhead, stick to the Western edge of this mountain range, return to trailhead in three days (maybe four) utilizing only low-tech gear (I will discuss low-tech gear in a future chapter), done! Not complex, but you have a simple course of action and it's a good idea to relay this to a loved one to make you and them feel good about your Earthroam.

Bottom line, *the plan* for an Earthroam can be as simple or complex as you make it. Again, you do you! I have conducted Earthroams where a friend has dropped me off at the foot of a mountain and with some words of encouragement, followed by a hug goodbye or a high-five. They know I will see them when I see them. Less is more, as eliminating a strict, confining plan allows for complete freedom and real connection to the land. Having sound survival and thrival knowledge accompanied by mastery of skills and abilities will help in the elimination of complex and overdone plans. Much of my success in Earthroaming stems from my survival and thrival skills I have spent a lifetime learning and mastering.

Nature Provides All.

Nature does provide all. For thousands and thousands of years, we have obtained everything we need from nature. The food we eat, the water we drink, the weather we experience, the soil we walk on – everything comes from nature. We are animals of nature. We are born from her, live within her and return to her one day. Nature provides more than just the physical outcomes, but actually provides the mental, physical, emotional, and primal connections all of us need, want and desire.

How a person mentally and emotionally connects to nature is for each person to discover on their own. Physically, some of us can understand that connection pretty simply, but others may take time and have needs that can vary from Earthroam to Earthroam. Nature's ability to provide opportunities to connect through various means is invaluable. This is an important part of an Earthroam; discover those connections and how they impact you moving forward with your life.

When on an Earthroam, if you consider that all you need is nature then she will provide for you. You are ahead of the game. Far too many times people play the *what if* game. What if we get lost… nature has many signs to point you in the correct direction. What if we run out of food… nature has millions of edible options for you. What if we are cold… nature will give her grasses and branches to warm you. The *what if* game could be played for hours with hundreds of *what if* questions and every can and will come from nature.

Seems like a bold statement to make, but our ancestors lived from and within nature far longer than anything else that has existed in the modern world. For hundreds of thousands of years, people of this planet obtained everything from nature. The proof of my statement is obvious. The modern world is young when compared to our ancient past.

We still need and desire the opportunity to live within the physical elements of nature as well as the mental, emotional, and primal components of nature. For me, an Earthroam is the best way to fulfill my mental, physical, emotional and primal connections to nature. When asked by people why I do it, why I Earthroam. My response is simple and the same; I hope to walk in with nothing and walk out with everything. Nature provides all!

That's it! Core concepts done. I told you I was going to keep this simple. I am not much for rules and regulations. Too much of that can stifle the minds creativity. As you move forward to reading this book keep referencing and really think about these core concepts. They are the four foundations stones all Earthroaming is based on.

Chapter 3

The High, Low and No

"Tell me and I'll forget. Show me, and I may not remember. Involve me, and I'll understand."

Unknown

When I say *The High, Low, and No,* I am not talking about the highs and lows of my time in the wild parts of the world. I am talking about the High-Tech, Low-Tech, and No-Tech Praxis (HLNP) of Earthroaming.

First, what does praxis mean? Praxis simply defined is the practice, execution or performance of a skill.

Second, what the hell is High-Tech, Low-Tech, and No-Tech? I am sure most of you can figure this one out, but here we go. High-Tech is short for High Technology, Low-Tech is short for Low Technology, and No-Tech is short for… wait for it… No Technology. These three technologies are the praxes (plural form of praxis) I Earthroam within. I Earthroam in a High-Tech Praxis (HTP), Low-Tech Praxis (LTP), No-Tech Praxis (NTP) or a combination of them.

Moving forward, let me break down the specifics of the HTP, LTP, and NTP. I want to add that these are not rules but categories I routinely find myself within while Earthroaming. More importantly, the HLNP will help shape your understanding on how I execute an Earthroam, allowing for you to better understand how you may conduct an Earthroam in the future.

- About 50% of the time, I Earthroam in a combination of an LTP and NTP. I might wear normal clothes, carry a stone blade, bring a friction fire set, a wool blanket, and a single-walled steel bottle.
- When Earthroaming within the NTP, about 25% of the time I will carry a stone blade, clay pot, animal hides for multi-use, wear a loincloth/breechcloth, wear animal skins, and create a friction fire set on the fly.
- When Earthroaming within the LTP, which is about 20% of the time, I carry normal clothes, a steel fixed blade, steel water bottle or billy can, a wool blanket, and I use a flint and steel in combination with char-cloth to make fires.
- When Earthroaming in the HTP (and this is not very often), I will carry a small lightweight sleeping bag or just a sleeping bag liner, multi-tool, steel bottle, a Ferrocerium Rod to light fires, and that is it.

The HLN Praxis chart provided gives a side by side comparison of the different Techs in the HLNP that I Earthroam in.

HLN Praxis Chart

High-Tech Praxis (HTP)	**Low-Tech Praxis (LTP)**	**No-Tech Praxis (NTP)**
Walled Tent or Multi-Seasonal Tent, Fabric	Canvas, Plastic Tarp or Netted Hammock	Hides, Robes, Cave, Leaf Bed, Rock Overhang

Hammock		
Multi-Tool, Lightweight Camping Axe, Folding Saw	Fixed Steel Blade, Fixed Saw Tomahawk, Woodsman Axe	Stone Blades, Stone Hand Axe, Stone Saw
Ready Meals, Freeze Dried Foods, MRE	Flour, Salt, Jerky, Rendered Fat, Sugar, Dried Fruits	Hunted, Gathered, Scavenged foods
Cook Set, Water Purification System, fork, knife spoon	Single Pot, Steel Bottle, Billy Can, Iodine Tablets	Wood bowl/shell/clay pot, boilability
Gore-Tex, Nylon, Fleece, Microfiber - Synthetic fibers	Cotton, wool, silk, jute, hemp, alpaca, mohair - natural fibers	Hides, Skins, Robes, Pelts, Leathers or Buckskin
GPS or Digital Map Software	Map & Compass	Sun, Stars, Weather - Natural Navigation
Sleep Systems or Sleeping Bag, Silk Bag Liner	Canvas/Wool Blanket/Bedroll	Hides, Furs, Skins - Natural Materials
Bank Line, 550Cord, Fish Line	Pre-made Natural Fiber Cords twine, hemp cord	Sinew, Silver Skin, Gut Sinew, Worked Plant Fibers
Rifle, Compound Bow, Crossbow, Slingshot,	Black Powder Rifle, Longbow, Recurve Bow	Stone Sling, Atlatl, Rabbit Stick, Self Bow, Spear
Headlamp, Flashlight, Fuel Operated Light	Oil Lantern, Candle, Oil Lamp	Fire, Rendered Animal Fat Lamps, Tinder fungus

Lighter, Waterproof Matches, Endless Match, Ferrocerium Rod	Flint & Steel, Char Cloth, Lens Magnification	Bow Drill, Hand Drill, Fire Plow - Friction Fire

To bring the HLNP into a full view, if you wanted to Earthroam within the NTP, the items in the far-right column may be on your gear list. Earthroams utilizing modern day gear and typical conveniences you will find in the HTP column.

What you choose and how you go about choosing it is totally up to you! Sometimes, I like to cross the lines and Earthroam within the NTP and LTP columns. I pick the best of both columns and go with it. Truth be told, you can bring whatever makes you feel comfortable and able. Again, these are not rules but just an idea as to how I execute an Earthroam. Maybe these will help you start thinking about how you could Earthroam as well.

The Big Four.

You may have noticed a trend when I was describing the percentages within the HLNP that I use. In every HLNP, I carry some aspect of a blade, blanket, bottle and burn (fire making). I call this the ***Big Four*** of Earthroaming. Making sure I have these four items is a routine for me when on an Earthroam. At times I will bring all four items or maybe just one and resource the other three from the land. Resourcing everything from the land can be tricky but totally doable with time and understanding. Sometimes, I will mix my Big Four in between the NTP and LTP. No matter the HLNP I choose, I aim to bring the Big Four or prioritize the acquisition of them if I bring nothing.

My Big 4 routine during any Earthroam mixed between the LTP and NTP looks like this; ***blade*** is steel or stone (I usually flip a coin to decide), ***bottle*** is single-walled steel to boil water and carry water, ***blanket*** is wool or an elk hide, and the ***burn*** is a locally sourced friction fire set. I know everyone and their mother has their own must have gear when practicing survival, bushcraft, or primitive skills. That's fine; you do you and let them do them. I am not practicing survival, bushcraft, or primitive skills; I am Earthroaming. I am just living.

All I can tell you is the more stuff you rely on to Earthroam, the less connection and freedom you will experience. I will put it to you like this; during any multi-day Hunter, Gatherer and Scavenger course I teach, the Big 4 are on the gear list – they are the only things on the gear list. Remember, this is one way, not the way, and that is how I Earthroam. Take what I have just shared in regard to the HLNP and the Big 4 and make it your own. One last thing… never substitute gear for knowledge, skills and abilities.

In late spring of 2017, I was asked to teach a three-day primitive skills course at an out of state survival school. I designed the course to cover primitive fire-making, natural navigation, stone tool technologies, glues and adhesives, primitive weapons, vessel construction, tracking, shelter-making, and all sorts of primitive camp craft. In all honesty, that is a great deal to cover in three days; however, I don't stick to an eight-hour schedule. I usually go sun-up to sun-down to maximize the daylight as well as the night for navigation using the stars. When teaching in the backcountry, every tree, river bend, rock structure, animal track, plant and sound can be a lesson. For this particular course I had four students and I knew I had plenty of time to cover all that was needed.

The four students came from all walks of life; one police officer, one doctor and two friends who owned a small bicycle repair shop together. A solid group upon first assessment that appeared to be motivated and ready to learn. The three-day primitive skills class would require us to walk out into the bush, survive, and thrive employing only primitive skills. No tents, no stoves, no backpacks, no water filters, no weapons… nothing. A good time for sure with the five of us, nature, and a ton of creativity!

Before any class I have a few routines that I like to conduct. First, we sit down as a group and discuss the tentative schedule. Everyone shares something about themselves and I answer any questions the students may have. Generally, we try to build a sense of group cohesion by getting to know each other. Second, I hold a quasi-gear inspection or gear survey to see what people packed, what they didn't pack, and address any questions pertaining to gear.

This particular class that day started the same way. … Keep in mind, weeks in advance and again two days before the class start date, I send a quick email reminding all participants of the gear list, which consists only of the Big 4. Not too complicated, really. But I also add that they can bring anything they think they might need. Not surprisingly, that statement typically leads to some interesting experiences.

"Let's take a look at what you all packed" I say.

"So, I brought a little extra," said the police officer. "I watched this YouTube video of this guy who is pretty popular in the survival community… he seems to know his stuff, so I packed what he recommended in his video."

"Good. Nothing wrong with that," I say. "It's *a* way, not *the* way… Now, Doc, if you don't mind me calling you that, what did you pack?"

"I packed some extras as well," said Doc. "I saw that you only required four items and thought I should play it safe with a few more."

"Same here," said the two friends in unison. "We didn't go overboard, but I think we have some baseline gear," said the older of the two friends.

"No worries gents. Keep emptying your stuff out and let's take a look at what you have," I said with a bit of caution and curiosity.

At this point, I witnessed four grown men empty well over a couple thousand dollars' worth of gear onto the forest floor. I was in complete shock. I saw collectively ten knives (not joking); six, maybe seven multi-tools; saws; different camp axes; complete mess and cookware kits; sleeping pads; blankets; sleeping bags; hygiene bags; an unknown amount of feet of 550 cord; flashlights; leg holsters with mini emergency survival kits; water filters; pounds of beef jerky; MREs; slingshots; and my personal favorite, a set of throwing knives.

I know I asked for this when I said bring anything you think you might need. I should expect folks to bring everything and anything, and I do. However, this is actually my first lesson.

"Outstanding gear everyone" I say. "I can tell you all are ready for anything and that is awesome. There is nothing wrong with being ready for, um, anything."

"That's what that guy says on YouTube – be ready" the police officer adds.

"I bet he does," I say.

"What did you bring, Donny?" Doc asks with an aspect of curiosity.

"Great question Doc… standby" I say.

At this point in time, I run to a small rock a few yards away where I have strategically cached my gear. I always do this. I always stage my gear a few feet away as this is my attention getter for this next lesson. Behind my chosen cache rock, I grab an old mountain blanket, called a Patu, that the men of the Hindu Kush would wear, a once steel-colored bottle now charred black from extreme use, and small three-inch fixed steel blade. I quickly head back to the mound of gear and my students.

"What the hell… that's it?" One of the friends say.

"In all honesty I don't…" the doctor starts to say.

"Before everyone freaks out, let's discuss" I say, trying to calm them down.

I explain that this is *a* way and not *the* way, but for this three-day primitive skills course, the blanket, bottle and blade that I am now securing to my belt will be the minimum gear we use. I do this for no other reason but to drive home a point that we are creative problem solvers and nature provides all our solutions. I have everyone stand next to their gear as I begin to call out different survival items and explain the way we will source and utilize that same item from the land.

"That 550 cord – grab it and put it back in your pack. Over the next three days, as a group we will make at least a hundred feet of natural cordage from different plant species that we will use for fishing and trapping," I say. "So, pack it away. We don't need it." This is usually the time when the light bulbs turn on and the smiles of excitement, concern and curiosity start to form.

"All your food, all your jerky and meals in a bag, pack those away. In the surrounding hills and forests there is a buffet of wild edibles, fish, and game that will be our sustenance the next three days."

"This is nuts. No food? I am not sure I can go three days without food," the police officer said. "Seriously, nothing?" the police officer said before being cut off by the friends.

"I am up for it… I think we got this" one friend says to the other and the group.

"If you need it, bring it," I say. "However, food – edible food – is all around us. Look down. Doc, you were wondering what I was nibbling on while waiting for you all to get your packs?"

"I was. I saw you reach down and start munching," he said.

"Correct, I did." At this time, I reached down and grabbed an unmistakable plant and held it up for everyone to see. "This is Oxalidaceae, or Oxalis, and it is one hundred percent edible." Without fail, every one of them picked a piece and popped it in as I did the same.

"It tastes…" the police officer trailed off.

"Sour," I said. "Fom the oxalic acid found in the plant, but it's commonly called wood sorrel and it is delicious… all 500 plus species of it," I said.

"There are 500-plus types of this plant?" the police officer said, still munching.

"Correct, give or take a few. We will not starve," I said with a smile. "Slingshots and throwing knives, pack them up. We will spend the next three days crafting all manners of primitive weapons to aid in our hunting efforts."

"Hell yeah, this awesome," said one of the bike repair shop owners. "I'm pumped to learn this stuff."

"I'm just glad I kept my receipts," said the doctor. "I think I might return a few things."

Fast forward three days and all five of us returned with no issues or mishaps. However, we did acquire quite a bit of gear during our time in the wilderness. Collectively we had five grass mats known as *back mates,* five bow drill friction fire sets, three hand drill friction fire sets, around 40 feet of natural fiber cordage, several rabbit sticks, one wooden walking stick per person (which also served as a thrusting spear), and several Paiute Deadfall sets, pre-made and ready to be employed. Additionally, we caught several fish, two rabbits, one snake, and an endless number of wild edibles. In the end we walked into the backcountry with next to nothing and walked out with a whole lot more.

You might think you need boat loads of fancy gear to Earthroam. I hope by now you're convinced otherwise. The beauty of Earthroaming in HNLP is that you can do whatever you want and create solutions from the world around you. Whatever praxis you decide to use, just remember that the core concepts of knowing more while carrying less, leading with curiosity, and holding a loose plan – if any – reign supreme over any tool you could pack. Nature provides all.

Chapter 4

Knowledge, Skills and Abilities

"The woods are lovely, dark and deep. But I have promises to keep, and miles to go before I sleep."

Robert Frost

To kick off this section of the book, you need to understand that I have been growing, refining, and mastering my knowledge, skills, and abilities for years. When Earthroaming, you're living. You are utilizing all your survival, bushcraft, primitive living and wilderness self-reliance knowledge, skills and abilities to live, and it's important to understand the difference between knowledge, skills and abilities. This is an important point, as many people group knowledge, skills and abilities into one term and use them as adjectives, but they are all different. Knowledge, Skills and Abilities are essential for any person who embarks on an Earthroam.

Knowledge is what you know, like facts, concepts, or theories. Take, for example, the fire tetrahedron: *fires start when a flammable or combustible material, in combination with a sufficient quantity of oxygen gas or another oxygen-rich compound, is introduced to a source of heat or ambient temperature above the flash point for the fuel and is able to sustain a rate of rapid oxidation that produces a chain reaction.* Knowledge is typically the information you find in manuals and textbooks. Knowledge is something you can cognitively recall, like knowing the Fire Tetrahedron or even Happy Birthday song.

Skills are things you do, like singing, rebuilding a car engine, throwing an atlatl. Skill requires technique to execute. When you put a skill into action, you will employ knowledge to execute the skill, like singing the Happy Birthday song on key and in time. To have mastery of a skill, knowledge and abilities must be mastered as well.

Abilities are natural or inbuilt. Abilities allow us to do something. Between skills and abilities, a fine line exists that determines if something is learned or innate. Abilities are innate traits or aptitudes that a person adds to a task or situation, like singing the Happy Birthday song with a naturally harmonized voice or throwing an atlatl with athletic precision. To put it in very simple terms, abilities are natural or innate whereas skills are behaviors which have been either learned or acquired.

For the most part, knowledge, skills, and abilities do not function independently. For instance, you're a bow hunter or archer, you may have the innate *ability* to keep your hands and arm in a steady position while acquiring your target, but a *skill* for shooting and hitting the target is what you learn from hours and hours of archery practice and study, which results in *knowledge*.

Like skills, abilities can also be sharpened and improved to a certain extent. For instance, you may have the skills to swim, but your ability to swim fast comes from possessing strong arms, back, and leg muscles, which you may develop with regular training, proper diet and exercise. This shows you can combine ability and knowledge to create skills which you can use.

Pay close attention when I use the words knowledge, skills, and abilities to describe Earthroaming. Even though knowledge, skills, and abilities are different in many ways I group them together into the acronym KSA for short. As you read ahead know that, for example, something like small game trapping could have several KSA associated with it. Just because I say, *small game trapping KSA* do not think of it is one or a single KSA. Believe me, for every KSA highlighted, there are several other KSA that are associated with it.

Every time I think of knowledge, skills, and abilities, my mind goes to a rock climbing outing I experienced a few years ago. I live in Colorado, and on this day a friend and I visited some local craigs to do some sport climbing and trad climbing routes. My friend and I have a depth of knowledge, skills, and abilities when it comes to climbing. We were a great climbing team. We knew each other's capabilities and limitations and we were always motivating the other to push it.

It was mid-spring, still cool when climbing in the shade, so we took a southern facing wall and climbed in the sun.

"Looks like we have some visitors coming our way," I said to my friend as he finished his climb. I gestured to a group of three climbers heading towards us.

"Looks like they had the same idea as we did to climb in the sun," my friend said with a chuckle.

I am not one to judge, but I am one to assess. The small group approached us and took up a position on a much easier climb right next to us. This climb was in the 5.8 range of difficulty and had some decent hand and foot placements. As I tied myself into my rope, I watched as they unpacked their gear. For the most part, the three climbers presented themselves in ways that would make anyone think they were knowledgeable in climbing. They were decked out in all the outdoor fashions and trends, had thousands of dollars' worth of climbing gear and equipment. One of them, the one who seemed to be the ringleader, spoke in climbing lingo using words like craig, runout, ascend, crux, chaussy and dirtbag. As a matter a fact he referenced himself as a *dirtbag* climber. Dirtbag is a term that some climbers use to describes themselves when they travel from place to place, climbing, living simply and without really worrying about anything except where their next route is. I started chatting them up and I asked them if they were local.

"I am local," said the ringleader. "They are from out of state and this is their first time climbing," He gestured toward the man and woman standing next to him. "This is my third time here. I have climbed some different craigs north of here. I just started climbing this year and spent quite a bit of time in the climbing gym, but now I'm making the transition to real rocks," he said proudly.

I turned my head, locking eyes with my friend. We exchanged a look that said *This could go terribly wrong.* We watched as the ringleader give some serious instruction to the two novice climbers. He covered everything from belaying, climbing commands, sport climbing techniques, how to put on the harness, shoes, chalk bag and helmet.

He was clearly knowledgeable, but I started to assess that he might not have the skills and abilities associated with his knowledge. I was concerned that the ringleader lacked the true skills and abilities to bring two novice, first-time climbers to sport routes that require more advanced skills and abilities to accomplish Not the best choice for first time climbers.

A climbing gym is a million times different than climbing outside in the environment. When you climb outside, you must contend with sudden weather changes, temperature swings, wind, loose rocks, plants, small critters inside hand holds, dirt and anything that a person could come across when being outside. I envisioned some kind of accident, and by the look on his face, my friend shared my concerns. No more than forty-five minutes later, the ringleader was stuck sixty feet up a rock wall, between two bolts with the top one having run out, meaning he was exposed to more danger because the anchor bolts were so spread out. He was mentally and physically stuck and in an extremely dangerous place. Our suspicions were confirmed. As the climber transitioned from providing his knowledge to the employment of his skills and abilities, we could see that his overall KSA was limited.

My friend and I quickly decided to get this guy off the face of the rock and assist the scared-as-hell newbie who was holding the belay. The ringleader was almost in tears, holding onto a huge jag of rock as a handhold for dear life. My friend belayed me while I climbed an adjacent route and talked one of the first timers through belaying the stuck climber.

"You alright, pal?" I asked while building a quick anchor in a small diagonal crack between and just above the ringleader and me.

"I was run out from my last bolt… I would take a serious whipper if I were to fall. I just freaked out," he said.

I finished my quick anchor build and secured myself to it. This anchor would serve as a new point of protection to secure myself and the climber. "Shit dude, you have to help me. Please!" the ringleader said, starting to panic. "My legs are toast. I feel like I'm going to fall."

"I gotcha man, just relax. I am going to fix you to this anchor, and you will be set." I said. Essentially, I built a giant pulley system that the belayers could control through the belay device, lowering the ringleader down. "The anchor has you now, let's get you down," I said "Slack!" I yelled down to the other two on belay.

"Slack! What the hell?" the climber said, "I'm going to fall!"

"Look man," I said with a bit of shut up and do-what-you're-told attitude. "I need a bite of your rope to run you through the anchor so you can get lowered down."

He relaxed. The first timer pulled the rope through the belay device with the coaching of my friend, removing all the slack from the rope.

Total time helping the ringleader was minutes.

"Down you go" I said. "Enjoy the ride."

"Thanks a million man. I bit off more than I can chew. Thank you, thank you, thank you!" he said as he was slowly lowered to the ground.

Knowledge, skills, and abilities are extremely important to have in life and in general, but especially during an Earthroam. I would not be able to do what I do today if I did not have the KSAs to do so. I take time to learn, practice, train and overall do the KSA associated with Earthroaming. KSAs can take a hungry day and feed you. KSAs can take a cold day and make you warm. KSAs can take a deadly situation and make it safe. In the upcoming chapter I am going to provide some concepts and KSA breakdowns that will help shape your future KSA development and you KSA requirements for Earthroaming.

Chapter 5

The Basics

"Life isn't about finding yourself. Life is about creating yourself."

George Bernard Shaw

Earthroaming doesn't require much in order to have a fun, adventurous and wild time. However, some basic ideas and concepts should be laid out for you so you can better understand my personal approaches and outlooks. The basics in this chapter are not to be a single source of application; instead, they are points of consideration into my pattern of life when on an Earthroam. Learn these, apply them, and re-work them into your own pattern of life when you decide to venture out into the wilds of the world on your first Earthroam.

Physical Abilities

Physical abilities are extremely important when it comes to Earthroaming. Being healthy is a must. Here's a little about me: at the age of 37, I had a massive heart attack, which doctors typically dub the Widow Maker. My left anterior descending (LAD) artery ruptured from a 99% blockage. I was extremely healthy. I didn't smoke, eat foods high in cholesterol and saturated fats, I never drank excessively or sat on my rear-end all day doing nothing. My LAD heart attack was genetics-based. It was my healthy primal lifestyle choices and the physical abilities that kept me alive and allowed me to recover quickly.

Far too many times I see survival, bushcraft, primitive, and wilderness self-reliance instructors, teachers and influencers lead an unhealthy lifestyle that is counterproductive to what they are teaching and preaching. I witnessed one survival instructor fail miserably during the demonstration of a bow drill friction fire. He lacked the physical strength and endurance to endure the bowing repetitions to create a coal. Yes, that is a tiring skill to perform, but lead and teach by example and not by words.

In Earthroaming, you must be physically fit. You are going to be testing your very own KSA in a real-life situation. This is not a *simulated survival scenario.* This is not a weekend *bushcraft camp out.* Earthroaming is the real deal, the real-life opportunity to thrive in an extreme situation. You will have to run, walk, swim, climb, scramble, and maybe snowshoe, ski, paddle, or bike every day for hours. You will eat far less than normal, endure a range of temperatures, and test every physical ability you have, every second of every day.

Earthroaming is a physical way of living and an extremely physical way of experiencing the outdoors. It should not be taken lightly but can be improved upon. If anything, physical abilities should be the first KSA to focus on. Without the physical abilities to make fire, your knowledge of fire is somewhat useless. Without the physical ability to build a shelter, the TOWERS concept of shelter building is of no value.

If you are a smoker, overweight, out of shape, indulge in unhealthy eating, conduct no physical training; all is not lost. Start now to make a change. Focus on the process of enhancing or changing your physical abilities instead of the goal at the end. Focus on the changes now that can support your current or future Earthroaming needs. I am not a personal trainer, but I am an

Earthroamer. My healthy lifestyle choices enhance my physical abilities to go farther and longer on my Earthroams, which allows for more freedom and curiosity-lead discoveries.

If you lack the physical abilities to Earthroam, I am not going to tell you what you need to do. You know exactly what needs to happen and what you need to do. Know that I support you and want you to experience the same adventures, discoveries, and amazing experiences I have, but only you can make that change. Make a difference for you. Make a change to become healthy, maintain a healthy lifestyle, and increase your physical abilities to Earthroam. Trust me… it is all worth it!

Creativity

Creativity is an ability that is extremely important in Earthroaming. Creativity is the number one survival and thrival skill. Nothing in this world would exist without it, and that includes us. Everything we come across is in some way, shape, or form a result of the creative process. Wait, isn't creativity learned? No, skill requires technique to be learned. Creativity requires no technique. A person can be creative and still have no skill or technique, thus making creativity an ability.

Creativity is the ability to take new and innovative ideas and turn them into reality. Creativity is classified by the ability to observe the world in new ways, to locate the hidden, to connect aspects of life that seemingly have no connection and to generate solutions. In its most simple form, it is thinking and then producing. On any Earthroam, thinking and creating is a constant. When we create new ideas and hesitate to act on them, we are only using our imaginations. We should all have a desire to bring something from our mind into existence. That is the essence of being human. For hundreds, thousands and millions of years, we have been employing creativity as the most important survival and thrival tool.

On any Earthroam a person could embark on, the ability to create – to think and then produce – is a daily or hourly occurrence. For me, the natural world around me impacts my creation. If the weather is changing from hot to cold, this will impact how I create a shelter. If I walk from one climate to another, like from a mountain top to a valley (they both have very different climates), elevation, moisture, and resources on hand will impact how I create my friction fire set.

I like to think that creativity is a survival skill that allows us to break the chains of conformity and create what we want, how we want it, and when we want it. So, what if you don't build the exact same shelter as everybody else? That's fine, everybody else lacks creativity and does what they are told! Did your shelter keep you warm, dry, and safe? Did you build a fish trap that caught fish? Did your snares yield a result? Did you get to create something from nothing? Yes? Congratulations, that is being creative.

As a flintknapper and primitive skills practitioner, I make stone tools. Hundreds of stone knives, blades, drill bits, arrow points, stone axes, atlatl points, stone saws, hide scrapers and stone ornaments. This is a passion and I have spent years mastering this skill. However, my mastery stems from my ability to be creative. When learning how to flint knap, I did not aim to replicate historical stone tools from cultures past. No! I wanted to create my own stone tools based on my needs, wants and desires. I focused on creating my own works of art that I could personally connect with, knowing that the stone tool I just created was the only one of its kind because I created it. I did not focus on making what others have already created, even though I can and have the KSA to do so, but I focused on what I could create. I imagined and then created.

When Earthroaming, the flames of creativity are burning bright. Sometimes the creativity applies to what we need right there and then, or what I call the *Primary Needs*. Primary needs can be building a shelter for the night, purifying water or treating a wound. At other times, we could focus our creativity on what I call *Secondary Needs,* which could include an idea for a book, or a solution to a financial problem, or even better, how you're going to build your house. They don't impact the immediate moment, but they do impact the big picture. Earthroaming ignites the creative forces to address the primary needs of the person as well as the secondary needs that can be acted on later.

Fire

The ability to make fire for an Earthroamer is essential – even lifesaving. Fire will cook your food, boil your water, keep you warm, ward off any unwanted visitors, aid in the signal for help, keep you entertained, and help you connect to the past. The KSA of fire making are endless and should be mastered. Far too many times I have witnessed survival students and survival instructors with impressive knowledge of friction fire methods and amazing skills and accuracy building friction fire sets fail miserably because they lacked the physical ability (they tire out) to create a small coal that would eventually become fire.

Always carry a fire kit of some type. I know I said that I often resource them from the land, but I want you to focus on the mastery of the KSA of your chosen fire kit. Your fire kit can fall within any of the HLNP. If you are in the NTP, maybe a hand-drill friction fire set organic to the area you are Earthroaming in is your fire kit of choice. If you are in an LTP, employ a flint and steel set that throws sparks into a local type of tinder fungus to start a fire. If you are in an HTP, utilize a ferrocerium rod as your fire starter. No matter how you are Earthroaming, master the fire making KSA specific to your fire needs.

I recommend that every Earthroamer strive and achieve ***one level of mastery for every HLNP (for a total of three).*** One High-Tech method, one Low-Tech Method and one No-Tech Method (See Fire Tech Methods Chart). Once you can make fire in all three praxes consistently and without failure, you must then create failure. What I mean by this is purposefully breaking, losing, reducing or creating an issue that you must overcome.

For example, let's say you have chosen the No-Tech fire making method of the hand-drill friction fire set. Using that set, you want to be able to routinely generate enough downward pressure, speed, and clean rotation to create a coal, place it into a properly constructed tinder bundle, blow it into flame, in various conditions every single time. This shows a level of mastery and routine execution of a skill reinforced through knowledge and abilities.

Fire-Tech Methods

High-Tech	**Low-Tech**	**No-Tech**
Storm Proof Matches	Flint & Steel & Char Cloth	Bow Drill Friction Fire
Ferrocerium Rod	Solar Refraction	Hand Drill Friction Fire
Ferrocerium Rod w/Striker	Fire Piston	Fire Plow
Magnesium Fire Starter	Standard Matches	Fire Saw

Electrical Heat Fire	Butane Lighter	Pump Fire Drill
Potassium Permanganate		

To create failure, you must create problems around the resources, conditions, and the physical components of the hand-drill friction fire set. This creates your troubleshooting procedures. In the case of the hand-drill friction fire set, let's create the problem of a windy day. How could you overcome it and make your fire? What about a broken spindle or hand drill? How do you overcome it? Do you find a new one? Do you use the floating technique on a shorter spindle? Do you use a spindle bit on a new spindle? Did you lack the hand control because of a shorter spindle?

Let's be honest. If the conditions, tools, resources are perfect all the time, then what level of mastery are you really obtaining? What and when are you truly learning? It's easy to have general KSA of several fire making methods, but when you master one, it is the start of mastery for all. Moving forward, master the KSA of fire-making for each HLNP, create failures, establish your troubleshooting procedures. Once you have full mastery of a fire-making method, move to another. Remember, mastery is not just making fire routinely, but creating scenarios where a true master of that particular fire-making KSA can work through any issues and create fire.

An Earthroamer should know the KSA of additional fire-making principles like tinder bundles, fire lays, carrying fire, protecting fire, using fire as a tool, signaling with fire, cooking with fire and using fire for protection. More importantly an Earthroamer should further advance their KSA by researching and understanding additional friction fire methods, chemical fire methods, solar fire methods, pressure fire methods and electrical fire methods.

Water

Water is the essence of life. All living things need it to live and thrive. When Earthroaming, water can become a driving force in day-to-day decisions. No matter the climate, water must be sourced and purified. We must have it and it has to be safe to drink.

The best and safest way to purify water is to boil it. Modern day water filters can also obtain a degree of purification that is safe to drink as well. Realize that *filtering* water is the removal of particulates (sand, dirt, leaves, solids, etc.) from water. This does not purify water, but makes it look cleaner. Additionally, if you are Earthroaming you might carry a water purification system with you. If you do so, most of your water problems as far as purification are over – now you just have to find it. The following water KSA is meant for the NTP and the mixing of NTP and LTP.

The exact time required to kill all waterborne pathogens (giardia, cryptosporidium, salmonella, HEP-A, cholera, etc.), viruses, bacteria, and parasites through boiling is still in question, as it seems everyone has their own opinion. The World Health Organization, The Wilderness Medical Society, and the Center for Disease Control all have different boil times. Ironically enough, they are all similar with a few, small differences in boil time and temperature ranges.

My recommendation: just boil it and *see* the boil! Let me explain why seeing the boil is so important. Water temperatures that rise above 160° F will kill all pathogens within 30 minutes and water temperatures that rise above 185° F will kill all pathogens within 5-10 minutes. So, in the time it takes for the water to reach the boiling point of 212° F from 160° F, all pathogens will be killed, even at higher altitudes. Makes sense, right?

But if I am on an Earthroam, I am not going to carry a thermometer… hell no. However, I know that water boils at 212° F. I can visually see the temperature of 212° F through the rapid boiling bubbles and steam released. This is my visual thermometer, and that's why *seeing* the boil is so important. People can argue all they want about how long you need to boil at 212° F, but once you see a roaring, continuous boil, you will know that all waterborne pathogens, viruses, bacteria, and parasites were dead in the 165° F - 185° F range. Can't argue with science.

Aside from sourcing water from the streams, lakes, and rivers around you and then purifying the water through boiling at a temperature of 212° F, an Earthroamer needs to be able to resource water for immediate consumption. This immediate water consumption source can come from above ground springs, below ground springs, wells, scratch wells, sip wells, fresh puddles, rain, fog, dew, snow, hail, ice, plants, and animals. To have the KSA to immediately source a purified drinkable water is invaluable.

An Earthroamer should possess the KSA of ***three immediate water consumption methods*** per season and the KSA of ***one filtering method per season***. Remember, filtering is the *clearing* of the water. No improvised backcountry, survival, or doomsday prepper water filter will purify water. It will make it clearer, but microscopic hazards can get through your design. None of the three immediate water consumption purification methods should require boiling water. Boiling water is a standard for the most part, and Earthroamers should look to master other KSAs dealing with the purification of water and the immediate consumption of it. Boiling water can fall in HNLP; however, using water filters is firmly planted in the HTP, while boiling water floats between the NTP and the LTP. The immediate water consumption KSA is based on the season because every season brings new challenges and opportunities to immediate water consumption.

An Earthroamer should aim to master seasonal, immediate water consumption KSA based on two principles: consumed from a direct source (drinking directly from a spring, puddle, or sip well), and collected and then consumed (collecting rainwater, sleet, snow, transpiration, fog in a tarp/cloth/sock, then drinking it). Bottom line, sourcing water and then boiling it is easy at times. However, an Earthroamer needs to be able to consume water on the move from immediate water consumption opportunities.

Lastly, an Earthroamer should possess the KSA to carry and store water. I have constructed wooden bowls, used animal skulls, made bush bottles, constructed tarp bottles and just about everything and anything else to carry and store water. This is when creativity comes into action. How would you carry fresh water from a spring to your camp if you did not have a bottle? How would you store purified water? How would you carry large amounts of water from one place to another? You have probably just imagined something in your mind… go create it!

Food

Food – the human crutch! Just joking. I know we need it. Not as frequently as water, but it is still something we need to run this amazing machine we call our body. Food is our main energy source. To better understand food acquisition during an Earthroam, I have broken the food into three frames of reference: Hunter, Gatherer and Scavenger. Additionally, if you are Earthroaming you might be bringing food with you. Food for thought: bringing food is an option, especially if it can supplement naturally collected foods. The following food KSA is meant for the NTP, and the mixing of NTP and LTP.

Hunter: An Earthroamer should have the KSA of both ***passive and active hunting*** methods. Passive hunting is best understood as fishing and trapping. I can build a fish trap, fish basket, trot line, or any other manner of fishing tool; place it into action; leave it for a time; and return to see what the yield is. It requires the KSA to build the fishing tool and then place it into action. Trapping works the same way; I can build any number of deadfalls, snare, pit, or swinging traps; place them into action; leave for some time; and return to see what the yield is. It requires the KSA of trap construction and trap employment. Passive hunting KSA might also entail, knots, cordage making, weaving, basketmaking, tracking, processing fish, woodwork, and small game.

Active hunting is pursuing prey on foot or baiting/calling prey into range to employ a weapon system to dispatch the animal. Active hunting requires countless KSA. I will list a few for you: tracking, improvised weapon construction and employment, game processing, food preservation, modern weapon employment, game calling, physical fitness, scent masking, camouflaging, and hunting blind construction. Active hunting is something that all Earthroamers should be extremely well-versed in.

***Gatherer*:** An Earthroamer can gather countless types of wild greens, flours, tubers, barks, fungi, seeds, stems, stalks, berries, mushrooms, and fruits for consumption or medicinal purposes. I have witnessed survival instructors on countless occasions list off numerous medicinal and edible plants to students that in no way, shape, or form is retained by the student. Literally, students melt with confusion and stress out over not knowing the plants their survival instructor just spit out.

I recommend to every Earthroamer to have the KSA to identify, source, and use at least ***eight different plants***, based on the season and the geographic environment they might be Earthroaming in. I call this knowing the *Straight Eight.* This is not about utilizing plants you already know or are familiar with. Don't incorporate plants into your Straight Eight like dandelions, Pine trees, cattails, Aspen trees, rose hips, thistles, purslane or any plant or tree you already know by sight, touch, taste or smell. Seek out new plants, seasonal specific, and organic to your Earthroaming area.

It is hard to remember hundreds of different tree and plant types. Start small, start with the Straight Eight and master them. Change your Straight Eight every year or six months and your KSA will grow. I like to stick to a year timeframe because plants based on the season have different tastes, colors, potency, shapes, smells, and identifiable attributes. If you only know what the plant looks like during spring, you could overlook or miss them come fall when on an Earthroam.

When picking your Straight Eight, I recommend that you identify ***three plants utilized mostly as food, two plants utilized as tools*** (cordage, sap, resins, vines, tinder, etc.), and ***three plants utilized for medical purposes*** (headaches, infections, diarrhea, vomiting, indigestion, etc.). This sub-breakdown of your Straight Eight will help you with the KSA associated with each plant. If you want to focus on edible plants instead of three different uses that fine… you do you!

Scavenger: An Earthroamer is the purest of scavengers. When we see it, we take it. We can scavenge from the dead, abandoned, or discarded as we need. An Earthroamer can scavenge animal kills sites for bones, sinew, or meat; nests with eggs, hives with honey, mounds for larva or eggs, and trash or debris we might come across only present future creative options. Even old or rotting corpses can be used for bones and rawhide for tool making. If its dead, abandoned or discarded, it belongs to the Earthroamer. Scavenging for insects (larvae, eggs, worms, maggots, etc.) is not gathering, but scavenging in my opinion. Effort exerted in scavenging is minimal, but the reward at the end can be amazing. Discovering an ant mound with luscious larva to scavenge is really based on chance.

The KSA associated with scavenging stem from what is ***dangerous to consume or possess***, along with the ***bacterial/viral impact*** the scavenged items might have on the Earthroamer. Caution should be taken; however, the KSA associated with scavenging must be mastered to avoid the spreading of disease, possible bacterial infections, and sickness. An earthroamer should assess that every scavenging opportunity could yield two results: a food to consume or resource to utilize. Not all scavenged sites are bacteria ridden and dangerous. A historical kill site from two years ago can contain the bones of an elk, for example, that are vacant of any tissue, fats, tendons or meat. This poses no real biological threat, but only offers countless opportunities to resource the bones.

The KSA for the Hunter, Gatherer and Scavenger are endless. On a macro level, when food is in question, the Earthroamer must have a mastery of the KSA associated with passive and active hunting methods, edible and medicinal plant identification drawn from the Straight Eight and scavenging for food and resources. They must also understand the risk vs. gain associated with them. Food comes in many forms and it is paramount that an Earthroamer have the KSA to harvest foods that can keep them physically, mentally, emotionally, and primally on track.

Shelter

Shelter is one KSA that every Earthroamer must be well versed in. Picking the correct location, utilizing the appropriate resources, and building a shelter based off the weather are all vital requirements. However, I don't break shelter-building into *types of shelters* an Earthroamer should know. Instead, I break shelter-building into a collective number of factors that will influence the type of shelter constructed.

Shelter-building can be one of the most creative aspects of Earthroaming. People discover building creativity and abilities when they break the rules of shelter-building conformity. Let's not restrict our creativity. Nature can provide so many different options and enablers that can take the standard debris hut and turn it into something amazing and long-term. Anytime I teach shelter-making, I do not stress the type of shelter made, but factors like Time, Occupants, Weather, Energy, Resources and length of Stay. I call this the ***TOWERS*** concept of shelter building. As I discuss the TOWERS concept of shelter-building you will find that many of the individual factors influence the others.

Time: Time is of the essence when on an Earthroam. When I say *time,* I mean two aspects of time: *how much time will it require to build,* and *do I have enough time to build it.* I have attempted to build shelters in the dark and I can tell you that I did more harm than good. Without the correct allocation of time to build and time left before the sun sets, tragedy can strike. When we don't consider time, it can and will be extremely difficult to build an elaborate shelter for multi-day living, or even something simple to get you through the night.

I believe time to be a very easy equation to solve. If I assess I need two hours to build my shelter, but I have only 30 minutes of daylight to accomplish it, then I need to rethink my shelter building options. Project ahead and allocate enough time to build based on your future actions of the Earthroam. This does not mean you cannot build once the sun is set. No, it means being considerate of time and the light available to safely construct the shelter. Additionally, time can refer to incoming weather. If I plan on building a huge, extravagant shelter, but severe lightning and rain is 30 minutes away, I clearly do not have enough time.

Occupants: The number of occupants is going to greatly influence the shelter constructed in a couple ways. For example, if you are conducting a Group Earthroam (Group Earthroams will be covered in a future chapter) with four people, your shelter must be big enough to house and safeguard four people from weather and any unwanted visitors that go bump in the night. This also means that you have four people to build the shelter and collect resources. Going back to time, the number of people can greatly increase productivity if time is running out.

Weather: Weather can be complex and multifaceted. Weather deals with current weather and future weather based on the duration of stay. If I see snow clouds in the distance, I will want to construct a shelter with excellent insulation, even though currently there is no snow. Weather elements influence and determine shelter locations and design based on wind force, wind direction, sunshine, visibility, precipitation, temperature, humidity, and cloud cover.

Simply put, the elements of weather are and always will be necessary for Earthroamers to battle against, overcome, or mitigate. We build shelters to reflect wind, block out intense sunshine, shield us from precipitation, help control our body core temperatures, and protect us from elements of weather. The saying, *location, location, location* is important, but here we mean weather, *weather, weather*.

Energy: Energy is best understood as the energy required to build the shelter and the energy required to live in it. We all understand that in order to construct a shelter, we will burn through energy stores in our bodies. Without proper energy, a shelter could cause more harm than good. I am sure many people have seen what I call the *human deadfall shelter*. It is a poorly constructed type of shelter with a main ridge pole that is weighed down to the point of failure, while a hopeless survivalist or bushcrafter sits underneath taking photos for social media.

Complete shelter failure is near in this case with a rebuild around the corner requiring more energy.

If I create a poorly designed shelter and fail to consider falling temperatures at night, I could spend the entire night shivering, attempting to heat my own body from my rapid movement. Then I would have to wake the next morning to gather more resources to improve my insulating layers on the shelter, thus burning more energy. If you properly construct a shelter the first time, you will avoid the over-expenditure of energy doing rebuilds and tons of maintenance. The same could also be said for shelters to block the sun create shade, or lower temperatures. If constructed poorly, the cooling effect will not take hold and cause the person underneath to lose more water, thus creating the need for expelling more energy to find more water. There is no perfect energy output solution. This is just a consideration point to think about.

Resources: In an ideal situation, you will have all and every type of resource available to build your shelter. Hopefully, they will all come from one immediate location; if not, maybe another area would serve you better. Having numerous construction resources (wood, branches, logs, grass, mud, clay, leaves, etc.) to build the physical shelter are key when selecting the shelter location. If I pick a perfect location to build a shelter, but have no resources around, I might want to rethink my location. Resources like firewood, fresh water, food options, natural sunlight, and safety (from animals, weather, and the natural environment) are additional resources that can impact the shelter construction and placement.

It's important to think about how some resources can be brought with you, depending on the Earthroam you are conducting. Never overlook resources like axes, saws, blades, etc. an earthroamer may have to construct the shelter, as well as tarps and hides that can be used for building materials. Even something like a hammock can afford capabilities and limitations.

Stay: The duration of your stay will greatly dictate the shelter build. Why build something elaborate when you are passing through an area? Duration of stay does not mean a shelter must be bigger, it just means it must last longer and must provide you with the requirements you need over a period of time. I have slept behind more giant rocks in piles of leaves than I have actual shelters. I keep it simple.

That is the ***TOWERS*** concept of shelters. Time, Occupants, Weather, Energy, Resources and Stay are all factors we must consider on an Earthroam. Never think that ***TOWERS*** is the way. It's simply *one* way of considering your future shelters.

Tools, Gear and Equipment: Tools, gear and equipment can be brought on any Earthroam to assist in the construction of a shelter. Tarps, trash bags, and plastic sheets all afford quick shelter builds and can most definitely save time and energy when used. Axes, saw, hatchets clearly will aid in chopping and cutting of wood for shelter construction. Rope, string and cordages can be a bonus. However, all the tools, gear and equipment I just highlighted can be sourced from the natural environment. Don't forget two of the Earthroaming Core Concepts: know more and carry less; and nature provides all.

Tools, gear and equipment are nice to have, but can create a nasty dependency. The saying, *all the gear and no idea-r* applies here, as people become so dependent on a tool or equipment that many *can't do* without. I am amazed when I hear students and instructors say, *If I had a (fill in the blank) I could (fill in the blank)* all the time. Learn how to source and make your own tools and you will truly be Earthroaming.

Natural Shelters and Structures: Natural shelters and structures are amazing and something I always seek to find on all Earthroams. Cautions when using some natural shelters ike caves should be taken. Many snakes, scorpions, centipedes, rodents, bats, bears, big cats, and ust about anything that can get inside, will make a home of a cave.

Check the area for bones, poo, dead animal remains, tracks, and anything that doesn't ook right or smells extremely bad. Caves are also subject to cave-ins and rock falls, especially if you light a fire in a cave. The heat from a fire can crack, split, and explode pieces of a cave, causing a cave-in. Check the floor of a cave for loose rock that have fallen as an indication of possible cave-ins or rock breakages. The cave floor is the best indication of what can fall from he cave walls and cave ceilings.

Many natural shelters and structures can be a small rock wall, rock overhang, a single boulder, stump, a mound of earth, downed tree or trees, or even a strange piece of terrain. Nature can provide anything. I view natural shelters and structures as work enablers. Imagine coming across a large boulder that creates a perfect windbreak. I would use it as it is – a wall that I *don't* have to build. I build a leaf and grass bed next to it, knowing the wind is blocked and no rain is coming, and then I crawl in for the night. Shelter done!

When it comes to shelters, be creative – that's the most important rule. Remember, nature provides all and can greatly assist by providing a roof or wall for a night. Shelters should be built for the needs and wants of you and your group. I could have listed off 50 types of shelters I have built and lived in. Yes, you could probably replicate them with ease. However, build your shelters following the TOWERS concept, and you can never go wrong.

Navigation

Navigation has been a lifelong passion of mine. I am often sought out to teach both natural navigation and good old map and compass navigation for other survival schools, military units,

Search and Rescue Units, and all manner of hunting guides. I truly love navigation and all it entails. With that being said, I always ensure that I do not navigate my way down a rabbit hole by sticking to Earthroaming Land Navigation KSA. When Earthroaming, we lack a hard plan which might stifle our creativity and curiosity. But I want to share with you some KSA for Land Navigation for the HTP, LTP, and NTP for when one is Earthroaming.

Natural Navigation: Natural Navigation is a must-have KSA for the Earthroamer. Keep in mind, natural navigation is the use of no equipment or gear to find your way. All direction-finding signs and tools come from the environment. Several books exist on the subject, but only a few are worth reading. Many, if not all, books cover improvised direction-finding methods, like sundials, shadow sticks method, analog watch direction finding, etc. These are useful, but again, nature will provide all. Establish the KSA of natural navigation and you can never go wrong.

The great part about being an Earthroamer is that I don't care where I am going as long as I am going. I know how to locate the North Star in the Northern hemisphere and the Southern Cross in the Southern Hemisphere, and what constellations rest directly above my house and some of my favorite caves. I use the constellations at different times of the year to help point me in the direction of home. My favorite trick is this: from tip to tip, the crescent moon points to the southern horizon when I am in the northern hemisphere.

These are a couple macro concepts that give me some cardinal direction. From drying puddles, tree roots, tree growth, warm rocks, cold rocks, ant hills, termite mounds, bird nests, animal dens, wind, weather, plant growth, and even moss, I can give myself the needed natural signs to find my direction of travel.

A very important aspect of Earthroaming is ***Sign Tracking***. This is a technique that I developed years ago and still use to this day. Sign Tracking is not navigating *per se* but recalling a route by the identification of signs. In Sign Tracking, the Earthroamer identifies macro and micro signs along the route from a 360° vantage point, signs that you can identify from close-up or farther away. Sign Tracking is best used in an Out and Back or Stay and Play Earthroam types (Earthroam types discussed in a future chapter).

The *signs* in Sign Tracking are fixed point, non-movable objects, or man-modified, fixed point, non-movable objects. A fixed-point object is a mountain peak, mountain saddle, river fork, or terrain feature you can recognize from more than one vantage point that will not move. Man-modified objects are trees with a small shape cut into opposite sides, or maybe even three sides.

Man-modified objects can be large boulders or rocks that can be leaned, stood erect, scored, or stacked. Cairns are a popular stacking method of stones and a great sign in Sign Tracking; however, do not place them where a person could purposely knock them over. Use some discreteness to mark a route with a cairn. A Sign Set is the combination of macro and micro signs a person uses to stay on their track.

A sign tracking route could look like this: This is an example of walking out to an unknown location (we are Earthroaming, after all, and we have… no real plan) and establishing a camp for one night, then using the sign sets to direct your movement back to your starting point.

Sign Set #	**Macro Sign**	**Micro Sign**
Set 1 Westerly (starting point)	Saddle in Mountain, snow on Northern Saddle	Leaning Cairn/triangle shape, white speckled rock
Set #2 Westerly Direction	Cross River at fork, head North	Across river "0" carved in tree directly at Fork

Set #3 Northern Direction	Walk through alley, hard cliff on West Side	Hard cliff with Leaning Cairn, One black rock, one Pink Rock
Set #4 Northern Direction	Aspen Grove, South side of stone Spire	Lightning strike Aspen
Set #5 (camp)	Stream on opposite side of Aspen grove	Small "X" placed on Jack Pine 25 yards from camp.

Sign Tracking can last for several days and have several Sign Sets. I use mountain peaks and valleys to control my movement and help guide me. If I tell myself to stay to the southern side of this mountain peak that is huge, well, I can easily go wrong. Instead, I pay attention to where I am going and use the fixed terrain features to help point my way home. I teach Sign Tracking to students from all walks of life, and you would be surprised how many fall completely in love with this technique to go out and back. Again, Sign Tracking works for a few types of Earthroams, but not all of them.

Using a map and compass in an LTP, or a GPS in an HTP, are all options as well. There's nothing wrong with utilizing digital or paper maps to help establish your position in the backcountry. If you are going to employ a set of tools, make sure you have the KSA for using them. Far too many times, I have seen the aftermath of poor navigation. I served in a Search and Rescue Unit at one point, and I can tell you first-hand that people with poor or no navigation skills become lost and even die. I have recovered bodies from deserts and mountains with maps still on their person. Having the full range of KSA for land navigation and natural navigation is a must for any Earthroamer, adventure seeker, backpack, hiker, climber, survivalist, backcountry skier, or anybody who may find themselves in the backcountry or even the big city.

Camp Crafts

Making camp crafts is where the Earthroamer creates tools and enablers to make their situation better or more comfortable. In no way, shape, or form should an Earthroam be miserable or uncomfortable. Having the KSA of camp craft will give many rewards to the Earthroamer. An Earthroamer needs to be savvy, creative, and skilled in camp craft. Below you will find some camp craft skills listed, with some examples of the crafts to be made.

1. Vessels: bush buckets, skulls, shells, bowls, wooden bottles, horns, bark containers, pots
2. Food Preservation: hot smoker, cold smoker, bush refrigerator, quick root cellar, salt
3. Cordage: reverse wrapped two-ply cordage, sinew process, bark cordage, roots, vines
4. Adhesives: pine pitch glue, hide glue, sap stickers
5. Weapons: rabbit sticks, spears, atlatl, stone sling, archery set
6. Trapping: deadfall traps, spring pole traps, swinging traps, pit traps
7. Netting: fish netting, trapping netting, storage netting
8. Baskets: food baskets, pack baskets, storage baskets
9. Tool making: stone, bone, wood
10. Clothing: sandals, buckskin clothes, breechcloth, shirts, ponchos, hats
11. Art: paint, dyes, brushes,
12. Sewing Kit: bone needles, buttons, cordage, awls, thread, sinew
13. Cooking: pot hangers, skewers, spoons, forks, ovens, meat smokers

14. Sleep: mates, blankets, pillows, nests
15. Light: torches, beeswax candles, rendered fat lanterns, fat candles, oil lanterns
16. Lounging: beds, chairs, stools, and mates
17. Luggage: packs, pack frames, storage bags, waist wraps, carry slings
18. Lithic Tools: blades, hand axes, stone arrow points, drills, stone atlatl points
19. Hygiene: soaps, brushes, washes, combs, sanitizers, cleansers
20. Instruments: drums, flutes, taps, sticks, hollows

Camp crafts are an excellent way to wind down after a long day, as well as create important resources for the Earthroam. However, camp craft can be for the pure enjoyment of creativity and not necessarily a priority. I often find myself making musical instruments, spoons, and items of comfort – like a brush or a hair pick – when time permits.

I spend hours sitting around a fire, sometimes in a cave or on an elk hide next to a fire, making cordage out of plant fibers. I can do it in complete darkness if needed, but cordage is the one thing I am always crafting at camp. I also focus on vessel making and weaponry. One of the first weapons I create is a rabbit stick. I have been using them for years and they are my number one go-to weapon. Camp crafts are endless. Get familiar with several and start working the KSA until you can do them in the dark.

Health

Today, it is very easy to seek a medical professional to aid you when you are ill or injured. On an Earthroam, it is more important to understand the ways to stay healthy. In simple terms, you must have the KSA to avoid illnesses and prevent injuries at all costs. Crucial factors like staying hydrated with adequate water, having enough of a caloric intake to run your body, obtaining enough rest, and practicing good hygiene are all crucial health factors.

Hydration is a must! Your body will lose water through natural processes like urination, sweating, defecating, and respiration. On average, adults can lose up to 2-3 liters of water a day during normal temperatures (between 65° F and 68° F). Anything below or above these temperatures can cause the body to lose water at a quicker rate. Extreme heat exposure, extreme cold exposure, intense physical activity, an increase in altitude, varying degrees of burns, and illness can increase the body's loss of water.

Dehydration is the outcome of a person's inability to replenish lost water. Once dehydration is in effect, simple tasks like working a knife, walking, speaking accurately, and executing a number of skills become difficult. Internally, the body's vital organs, like the brain, kidneys, liver, and heart, start to shut down. The only way to treat dehydration is to replenish lost body fluids. On an Earthroam, consume any potable water or liquids you may have. Again, knowing how to locate and source immediate water consumption sources can save your life. To avoid dehydration, look for early signs:

BODY FLUID LOSS %	**RESULTS**
4% - 8% Loss	Thirst, nausea, weakness, fatigue, irritability, tender joints, cramps
9% - 11% Loss	Decrease of fine motor skills, dizzy, intense headache, numbness in limbs

13% - 15% Loss	Loss of vision, painful urination, swelling of tongue, swelling of joints, loss of hearing, feeling of numbness across body
15% + Loss	Vital organ failure or death

Energy in the form of food provides necessary calories to run the human body. Having adequate food can turn any Earthroam from a day in the backcountry to a week or more in the backcountry. Food will keep you healthy. Yes, we can go for long periods of time without it, but this does not mean we are healthy. Without food and the caloric energy it provides, we become weak. Food provides important vitamins, minerals, fats, salts, and sugars that are all essential for our body to properly function during an Earthroam.

Additionally, food provides a boost of morale. It provides physical, emotional, mental, and primal connection to the earth, yourself, and the group of people you are Earthroaming with. Aside from the caloric energy it provides, food makes everyone feel better. Many cultures around the world base their day around a single meal that brings community and family together. Apply that same idea to an Earthroam and you will discover a new approach to food.

Rest is extremely important when Earthroaming. Rest in the form of sleep, or simply taking a break, can restore our mental and physical abilities. We need to sleep to recover, heal and fortify our bodies. When we deprive ourselves of sleep, we lose focus, become irritable, and are more accident-prone. I am sure we all know people who become emotional and chaotic if they are not well-rested.

During an Earthroam, I rest and sleep all the time. I never overlook sleep and I enjoy finding the most off-the-wall places to sleep. My body needs it! Rest is a requirement for most living things on this planet. On an Earthroam, lack of rest alone can turn your experiences from good to bad, or bad to good when you have it. Remember that when you Earthroam, you need no plan, so when you are tired, feel free to sleep. It is ok to make the spot you napped in your home for the night.

Hygiene; as silly as it sounds, this can make or break you on an Earthroam. Hygiene will prevent infection and disease. You must keep yourself clean in some fashion. Depending on the Earthroam you are executing, you could bring soap. To be honest, bringing a bar of environmentally safe soap could make all the difference in an Earthroam.

My methods of hygiene are different than some, but they work extremely well. Every 5-7 days I conduct a Creek Dunk. I jump into a creek naked and wash using water and sand river stone to scrub my body of dirt and grime. If I have no creek, I will airbathe or sunbathe. I strip naked and stand in the sun and let the air move across my body. This dries my skin and exposes my body to the sun. I will also conduct a smoke bath. I light a fire, add some naturally good-smelling green plants or flowers, and let the smoke poor over and through me while standing naked. This will help with any fleas, parasites, or bacteria on my body or hair.

I always clean my hands with water or plants that have a cleansing and soapy effect. I scrub my hands with sand or small stones to remove dirt and grime. I wash my clothes when they are dirty. I use a creek or some type of water source and dunk and scrub them until they are clean. Just work the clothes between your hands and they can become surprisingly clean. I scrape my teeth around the gumline with soft, fibrous woods and plants to prevent mouth ailments. I drink teas that help fight mouth ailments, as well. I also check my feet when wearing shoes or sandals or when going barefoot. I wash them the same way I would my body, and never pop blisters.

You will stink at times, your clothes will have odors, and your hair and nails will become nasty as anything; however, you can still clean yourself to prevent illness or infection. Keep it simple or learn how to make soaps from rendered animal fats, wood ash, and plant ingredients. Either way, you must practice good hygiene and keep yourself clean.

That's it; these are really simple concepts and methods to consider when Earthroaming. Like I mentioned before, this book is not a survival manual. I didn't want to list out hundreds of traps that don't really work, nor did I want to provide you some strange and obscure methods of purifying water that will make a billy goat sick. With these basic methods and ideas, you'll be able to think about how the natural world can provide, and you'll know the important factors to consider when Earthroaming.

Chapter 6

Earthroaming Environments

"Study nature, love nature, stay close to nature. It will never fail you."

Frank Lloyd Wright

An environment is the domain and conditions in which plants, animals and humans find themselves functioning. Think of a fish tank. The fish in the fish tank live and function within that fish tank environment. During an Earthroam, a person could find themselves in many different environments or just one. In this chapter, I would like to discuss different Earthroaming environments, examples of them, advantages and disadvantages of each, along with some best practices to operate within them.

Remote Environments

Remote environments are my favorite. Simply defined, remote environments are large, vast, open areas of earth with no human footprint or impact. Think of the Amazon Jungle, deserts of the American Southwest, or the mountains and valleys of the Rocky Mountains. Like many people, I crave the isolation, the openness and the ability to connect with nature in its purest and raw form. I love the challenge and experiences I encounter when Earthroaming in a remote environment.

The benefits of Earthroaming in a remote environment include the ability to truly let curiosity guide you from place to place with no interference from external factors (cars, buildings, people, etc.). In a remote environment, an Earthroamer can apply and test their survival, bushcraft, primitive and wilderness self-reliance KSA. Creativity becomes an essential ability because the Earthroamer is stripped of modern conveniences at times and must think and then produce what is needed. Lastly, people can and will discover why a remote environment Earthroam is beneficial to them. On a macro level, the more remote the location, the more I can feel isolated, connected, tested and rejuvenated. In no other environment can I find the same when compared to a remote environment.

The disadvantages of remote environments are the isolation and lack of modern medical resources if the Earthroamer becomes injured or sick. These environments also pose new challenges with respect to weather. Flash floods, mud slides, lightning strikes, temperature swings, forest fires, blizzards, hail, fog, rain, sandstorms, all fall with the environmental hazards of the remote environment. Wild animal encounters and poisonous plant exposure can be life ending if the Earthroamer lacks the KSA to identify, prevent, and overcome encounters.

In today's world, many types or remote environments exist.

Rural Environments

Rural Environments are areas of land that have a low population density, with very few homes and buildings. They are usually found outside of cities and towns. Within a rural environment, people typically work on farms, ranches or small settlements. When we think of a rural environment, places in Canada like a fishing village come to mind, or small farming communities in West Texas, or even a small agricultural forestry center in Alaska. Most rural ıreas are comprised of large open areas, forests, deserts or aquatic habitats (lakes, streams, ivers, etc.) with very little people and little infrastructure.

An important point to consider is that many rural environments eventually become emote environments, because rural environments often sit along the edges of remote nvironments. This is common in many places around the world, but not a constant. Conduct ome initial research before you Earthroam to better manage your expectations about how the and is allocated between a rural environment and a remote environment.

The benefits of Earthroaming *near* or *around* a rural environment is the ability to receive imited help if needed. One can still obtain the ability to truly let curiosity guide them from place o place with no interference, if you avoid the rural area or settlement. In a rural environment, an Earthroamer can still apply and test their survival, bushcraft, primitive and wilderness self-eliance KSA with few restrictions, aside from directly interfering with the daily happenings of he rural settlement, farm, or village. In a rural environment, an Earthroamer can do much of vhat could be conducted in remote environment with a few limitations.

The disadvantages of Earthroaming near or around a rural environment are the encounters etween people, livestock and just about anything else. This is a compromise of your Earthroam f you are attempting to isolate yourself. Rural environments draw lines in the sand as far as oundaries and property markers, which could impede your forward progress and stifle your uriosity. Illegally crossing into someone's property or territory, and then getting caught could ose serious issues from fines or penalties to being shot at, or even beaten up and robbed. People lay by a different set of rules in rural environments.

Suburban Environment

I almost never Earthroam in suburban environments. I find myself at times passing through them or avoiding them at all costs, but they are still an environment an Earthroamer could encounter. A suburban environment is best defined as a mixed use of residential and commercial areas on the outskirts of a city or large town. To better understand what a suburban environment is and looks like, most people just have to walk out their front door. It makes sense as most people today live near a city or large town in the suburbs or burbs.

Advantages of Earthroaming in a suburban environment do exist, but they are based on the person and their needs, wants and desires. Again, Earthroaming has no special rules. If you start your single-day Earthroam in your local suburban environment and walk a trail into a rural environment, you can still let curiosity guide you and absolutely have an awesome time doing it. Good for you. You do you! What else could you ask for? If that suburban environment is your pattern of life and you have no desire to seek other environments...grow where you are planted!

An Earthroam that passes through a suburban environment can afford many advantages based on the type of Earthroam (I will discuss Earthroam types in the next chapter). The suburban environment can provide modern medical services if the Earthroamer is sick or injured. The suburban environment can also provide the Earthroamer the opportunity to shower, restock on food supplies, communicate to others if necessary, dispose of trash, end an Earthroam or initiate another leg of an Earthroam if needed.

The disadvantages are obvious: if you are trying to isolate yourself and connect with nature, it will be much harder to accomplish those goals in a suburban environment. Suburban environments can be costly, time consuming, and a distraction to the Earthroam. If an Earthroam passes through a suburban environment, the Earthroamer must make note of local pedestrian traffic laws, motor vehicle traffic laws, curfews, enforcement officials, and any number of local rules and restrictions that are in effect.

City Environment

City environments can be very complex at times, but in all actuality are their own type of Earthroam. I will discuss the specifics of a city Earthroam in the next chapter. The definition of a city environment is a large human settlement. What usually separates large cities from smaller cities are housing, transportation options (trains, subways, busses, etc.), sanitation utilities, medical services, higher echelon educational institutions, government buildings, museums and communication infrastructure. I am sure everyone is familiar with major cities like New York City, London, Tokyo, and Los Angeles, and I don't need to go much further than that.

Advantages of a City Environment are amazing, as they actually have similar advantages to a remote environment Earthroam. Many people today crave the hustle and bustle of a city. The noise, smells, tastes and atmosphere of the city allow for the ability to connect with the city and other people. For some people a city environment is their preferred environment. A remote environment is my ideal Earthroam, but to someone else, the ideal Earthroam may be a city environment. A city is a social environment and people crave social interactions. I am not naturally drawn to the city environment, but the challenge and experiences a person could encounter when Earthroaming in a city environment are endless.

The benefits of Earthroaming in a city environment include the ability to truly let curiosity guide you from place to place with literally thousands of new places and experiences to discover. In a city environment, an Earthroamer can apply and test their *Urban Survival* (I hate the term Urban Survival, which I think is very misleading and inaccurate), City Survival and City Self-reliance KSA.

The disadvantages of city environment Earthroaming are endless and could literally be their own book. However, I will list a few that can and will apply to most city environments; pollution, crime, riots, violence, protests, misinterpretation of laws, political indifference, sociological issues and cultural prejudices. Now this is not the case everywhere, but it's common this day and age. Don't conclude that a city environment is wrong and an evil place, but just accept that it is an environment in which you may face a different kind of challenge.

Earthroaming Environments Best Practices

1. Remote environments require advanced survival, bushcraft, primitive, and wilderness self-reliance KSA. Know what you are doing, or it could cost you your life.
2. In remote and rural environments. let someone know where you may be Earthroaming. This could help a Search & Rescue Unit locate you should you need it.
3. When crossing personal property lines or boundary markers, ensure you have permission from a landowner or property management facilitator.
4. Know all hunting, trapping, fishing, foraging, fire-making and weapons rules and regulations you may Earthroam in or through.
5. Pack out whatever you pack in. Leave it better than you found it.
6. If you find yourself on your Earthroams crossing into different environments in a different country and plan to resupply, have local currency.
7. All Earthroaming environments require great physical conditioning and health.

8. All Earthroaming environments require excellent situational awareness and common-sense tools. Trust yourself, as you are typically correct the first time.
9. Check equipment and gear before departing. Don't wait or it could be too late.
10. Murphy's Law is in full affect when Earthroaming. If something can go wrong, it will, and usually at the worst time.
11. Based on the environment, know basic self-aid and first aid skills, or where to go in the event of a medical situation.
12. If Earthroaming in a group or small party; know the capabilities and limitations of everyone in the group, paying close attention to how those could play out in the environment.
13. In all Earthroam environments, be aware that what goes into your body is eventually going to come out. Know how and where you can go to the bathroom.
14. In a city and suburban environment, mirror and match the civilian population as much as possible to avoid confrontation and unnecessary encounters. Don't walk through a city with your primitive bow and hand drill friction fire set... problems are bound to surface.
15. Spend more time in the environments you connect with and less time in environments you don't connect with. If it doesn't make you happy, don't do it!
16. When Earthroaming in foreign countries and foreign environments, know the local customs, courtesies, and dress. Also know the basics of the local language.
17. Remote environments will keep you isolated, and city environments will expose you; be ready to deal with anything that could come your way.
18. All Earthroaming environments require the Earthroamer to be weather wise and be able to identify indications and warnings of weather extremes or incoming adverse weather.

19. Let curiosity guide you in every Earthroaming environment.
20. Make your Earthroam work for you no matter what environment you are in.

Something to consider when Earthroaming is the possibility to encounter several different environments. Take any person who has hiked the Appalachian Trail or the Pacific Crest Trail. They can attest to the number of mixed environments they encounter. I have spent many days on both trails and can tell you that one hour you can be remote as can be and a few hours later you can be eating ice cream and hotdogs in a town's local convenience store. Be prepared and ready for anything when changing environments.

Do your homework before you Earthroam! Make sure you are prepared to have no plan, as funny as that sounds. In all seriousness, if you are traveling to a different country, territory, state or province and heading to the more remote environments in them, make sure you have the KSA of the different flora, fauna, indigenous groups, borders, environmental threats and just about everything you might need to know. Educate yourself and reduce the possibilities of accident, death, or embarrassment. Know before you go, because what works in one environment will not always work in another.

Chapter 7

Types of Earthroams

"Nature is not a place to visit. It is home."

Gary Snyder

I have conducted many types of Earthroams all around the world and I can tell you they are uniquely different in some ways and similar in others. In this chapter, I will break them into individual *types* and discuss some specifics for each one. It's important to remember that Earthroams are not guided by rules or concrete plans, but by curiosity. The following types are for you to better understand what you may experience on an Earthroam.

Walk Back Earthroam. A Walk Back Earthroam is just that: I walk back. I routinely get dropped off at a location by a friend and walk back home. Often, the ending is my personal residence or someone else's personal residence. Sometimes a Walk Back Earthroam can be walking back to a location where your personal vehicle is parked or cached. Time is not a factor in a Walk Back Earthroam because nobody is waiting on you. You get back when you get back. You get dropped off at location and walk back to whatever *back* is for you.

During a Walk Back Earthroam, be prepared to crossroads or major thoroughfares and even pass through small towns and cities when walking to your *back* if you live in any area aside from a remote environment. Additionally, consider what might be on your person (knives, weapons, plants, wild game, etc.) and could draw unnecessary scrutiny from passersby and raise suspicion on behalf of authorities. Many times, I have been misidentified as a vagrant or homeless person after walking back to my house after a multiday Earthroam. It happens but be prepared to explain yourself if that happens.

Out and Back Earthroam. An Out and Back Earthroam is explained in the name. I walk out from a location, letting curiosity guide to wherever it leads me, turn around when I am ready, and walk back to where I started or a completely different location. An Out and Back Earthroam could take three days or 30—it is entirely up to you. Like the previous type of Earthroam, the *back* does not necessarily have to mean where you started. Again, heed my warnings that the perceptions of people can be ruthless; do not be surprised if someone reports you when you are attempting to return to your personal residence or friends' residence.

Stay and Play Earthroam. A Stay and Play Earthroam is where I walk to a place and just stay. I stay in one place because I want to play. When I say *play,* I mean; hunt, fish, trap, eat, skinny dip, sunbathe, scavenge, work on crafts, connect, or just be. Simply put, I have found my dream location or oasis of the world and don't want to leave. Everything I could possibly need exists in the now and present. Why leave?

A Stay and Play Earthroam could be a single day to several days. A stay and play Earthroam is great because you are not relying on anyone to drop you off or pick you up. You can encounter far more freedom and opportunities. I like to use my stay and play location as a hub for daily Earthroams to discover and explore, but each night I return to my location. A Stay and Play Earthroam is something great to do in small groups, or even with family members that might not want to spend thirty days in the backcountry.

Rendezvous Earthroam. A Rendezvous Earthroam is where I am going to rendezvous with a person at a specific time and place. The issue with a Rendezvous Earthroam is that you are now bound to another person's schedule and personal considerations. You can find yourself losing out on connections, opportunities for creativity, and the chance to be led by curiosity because of a rendezvous plan. I know, no real plan is the preferred way to Earthroam, but sometimes when other parties are involved, you must consider them and do a little coordination and planning.

The rendezvous location can be any place that you and the other person can identify and get to. A good Rendezvous Earthroam will have a window to allow for both parties to flex time if needed. For example, let's say the rendezvous plan is for you to leave on Wednesday and rendezvous on Monday, five days later at 12:00 noon. Work into the plan that if neither party shows Monday at 12:00 noon, shift the rendezvous pickup time 24 hours later to Tuesday at 12:00. If that is missed, shift the rendezvous pickup time 24 hours later to Wednesday at 12:00 noon. How many flex days you have is up to you and the other person, but the flex does give some opportunities to connect, create and lead by curiosity.

There is the possibility that you or your friend does not show up due to some unforeseen circumstances and the entire process is delayed. If this was to happen, a good contingency plan activating a personal recovery plan should be in place. This plan will have to be enacted by your friend, your "pickup," if you do not arrive on time or even at an alternate time. I have never had that happen to the extent of becoming injured and missing a rendezvous, but it does not hurt to have something in place for the sanity of your pickup friend.

Pick Up Earthroam. A Pick Up Earthroam is almost like a Rendezvous Earthroam, but I will initiate contact via phone (my cell phone, someone else's cell phone, pay phone, store phone, police phone, etc.) through a text message or phone call. Basically, I am contacting someone who has previously agreed to pick me up to let me know that it is time to pick me up. This type of Earthroam works great in areas you don't personally reside in (out of state or country), but have friends or family in an area to facilitate the pick up. This style of Earthroam gives way more freedom and opportunities to the Earthroamer, because the Pick Up Earthroam is more of an action than a plan and affords major flexibility to everyone.

The downside of a Pick Up Earthroam is that you have to have a phone or find access to a phone. This can be troublesome as phones die and charging one on a multi-day Earthroam is almost impossible, unless you bring some charging capability. Additionally, most people will not lend a person their phone who is stinking, dirty, bearded, probably has a blanket tied around his waist, a knife shoved down his belt, some type of primitive fire making tools in his right hand and a dirty bottle of freshly boiled stream water in the other. So, work out a general course of action... or just wait, the police will eventually show up and they typically have a phone.

Mixed Mode. A Mixed Mode Style of Earthroaming is taking the Walk Back Earthroam, Out and Back Earthroam, Stay and Play Earthroam, Rendezvous Earthroam, Pick Up Earthroam and working in a mix of different modes of transportation and Earthroaming style. Maybe your Earthroam is water based. For example, you were dropped off at a kayak put-in location where you will start to kayak down the coastline and intercoastal waterways. You stop along the way at various points of curiosity and interest. You Earthroam inland from your last point of interest conducting an Out and Back style trip, eventually returning to your kayak where you continue with your Mixed Mode Earthroam only to be picked up, a few days later when you are finished.

The Mixed Mode style of Earthroaming can encompass modes of transportations like mountain bikes, snowshoes, cross country skis, dog sleds, canoes, and kayaks. It is easy to use these modes of transportation in all styles of Earthroaming with the appropriate KSA. Even in a City Environment with planes, trains, subways, boats, ferries, bicycles, pull-carts and automobiles an Earthroamer can use these modes of transportation when conducting a Walk Back Earthroam, Out and Back Earthroam, Stay and Play Earthroam, Rendezvous Earthroam and Pick Up Earthroam. I have conducted Mixed Mode Earthroams where I cached my mountain bike beforehand and rode home later.

In January of 2014 a nice snowstorm was expected to hit in some of the mountains I Earthroam in frequently, so I jumped at the chance to push the normal limits of an Earthroam. I decided to conduct a Rendezvous Earthroam with a good friend after the snowstorm ended. I was going to leave several days before the snow came, have the snowstorm hit and the rendezvous with my friend several days later in a small town where he would pick me up, for a total of seven to ten days—nothing crazy.

My gear list included one mylar emergency blanket, tomahawk (my blade), bottle, thick wool blanket and a pair of snowshoes. I was wearing a pair of outdoor pants with long johns underneath, a long sleeve shirt and a Baja Hoodie. Not much, but just enough to get the job done. I fell somewhere between the HTP, NTP and LTP; the best of all worlds during this winter Earthroam.

EARTHROAMER

This Earthroam was awesome! I made an amazing friction fire set that lit many fires, lived in some amazing caves, ate rabbits, snowshoed for days, built some snow shelters, found a young mule deer that was killed by a predator and cut some meat from it (totally frozen) and took some bones, made a wooden bowl and drank beef and bone broth from it. I made some amazing rabbit sticks that I still have to this day, all while inch after inch of snow fell to the ground. Curiosity led, and nature provided all. I did not have a plan, but I knew more so I carried less.

All that awesomeness worked well in the mountains, but in the civilized world, roads were snow packed and dangerous, temperatures were well below freezing at times, people were stranded on roadways, and an overall sense of chaos took over the area where I lived. The day came when I was supposed to rendezvous with my friend at 9:00 on the outskirts of this small town near my home. A constant shower of snow fell to the ground when I woke up early that morning from a small improvised shelter, I had built the afternoon before. I threw on my snowshoes and headed to the edge of town to rendezvous with my friend.

On my walk into the small town the snow intensified, and it eventually became a white-out. I struggled to walk through the conditions but made my way to the edge of town where the snow cleared a bit and where I was supposed to meet my friend. It was well before 9:00 am in the morning and the day was just starting. I could tell from spending so many days Earthroaming in the mountains that it was somewhere between 7:30-8:15 am.

I waited and waited for my friend as the snowfall intensified and came down now with fatter flakes. I positioned my myself under a big pine tree to block some of the wind that had increased its intensity and keep my eyes on the road. My wait continued as the snow intensified and as the wind blew harder and harder at every passing minute.

"It has to be at least 9:30... where is he?" I said aloud. "Maybe I need to start bringing a phone." I continued to wait and was on the verge of heading back into the mountain to find a quick shelter for the day and night when headlights became visible in the distance down the road.

"This has to be him... finally," I said with a completely frozen breath. The lights on the car grew bigger as the distance between the car and me decreased. "It's totally him... hell yeah." I slowly emerged from under my pine and made my way to the edge of the road to quickly discover the lights on the car that I believed to be my friend's really belonged to a police vehicle. Funny enough, the officer turned on his other lights just to prove he was a police officer. I stood motionless and hoped the police officer would just drive by in response to something else, but the red and blue lights stopped exactly where I was standing.

"Officer," I said. "What can I do for you?" as he rolled down his window.

"What are you doing? You alright?" he asked a little rudely, with a sense of genuine confusion.

"Just out for a hike and…"

"A hike? Do you have identification? What are you doing out here?"

"No... I don't have any identification and I am waiting for my ride."

Now, I am not trying to be intentionally vague, but I knew this cop was not going to get out of his car and was going to do his due diligence checking out the bearded, snow covered, Baja wearing, Yeti looking monster standing on the side of the road and then be on his way. I was not giving a hard time to the police officer, but I didn't have any identification.

"You have no identification," he said.

"Nope... don't carry ID on me when I am out hiking. As a matter of fact, I don't carry much with me when—"

"So, then I will ask you one last time, what are you doing here?" the officer said with more of an authority, but I could almost hear the undertone of please *don't make me get out of this car...its freezing.* I decided to lay it all out on the table and see how it played.

"Ten days ago before the snow came my friend dropped me off with a wool blanket, tomahawk, snowshoes, metal bottle, emergency blanket, and the clothes on my back to Earthroam through the mountains until this very day when I would meet him at 9:00 am." I could tell by the look on his face he thought I was telling the truth, or I was high, maybe extremely high. "I am assuming it is past 9:00 am. He's late, probably because of the snowy conditions, so I was just about to head back into the mountains when I saw a set of headlights coming down the road, your headlights and thought it was him."

"Wait... so you have been out in the mountains for the past two weeks?" the officer said with some curiosity and disbelief.

"That's correct officer."

"You didn't have a tent or anything?" he said in disbelief.

"No tent, but I had a few items... all the ones wrapped up in the blanket now covered in snow," I said with a chuckle.

"You're insane. I mean, you are truly insane. Aren't you cold?" he asked.

Our conversation continued for another minute or two before I supplied him with name and address. We chatted about the town and random stuff. I know the police officer was doing a quick vetting and validation of who I was, so no issues there, but not once did he offer to give me a ride or let me warm up inside his vehicle. As I was supplying him with where my kids attended school and my favorite local eatery, I saw another set of headlights approaching slowly.

"I see another set of lights coming... hopefully it's not backup?" I said jokingly.

"That's not one of my guys. Hopefully it's your friend."

The officer watched the car approach in his rearview and I stepped back from his warm window to get a better look. As the lights came closer, I could see it was my friend Matt. I figured he saw the flashing lights and me standing there looking like a snow-covered Yeti and put two and two together pretty quick. Matt pulled up next to the police officer's car, rolled down his window as I gave him a wave mixed with a grimace.

"I don't know him officer…put him in jail," Matt said.

"Shut it... thanks for coming out in this, dude," I said. "I didn't think you were going to show."

"Sir, is this your friend?" the officer said.

"Yes... an insane one to say the least," Matt said with a smile.

"He is insane. I can't believe you go out in this," the officer said, still in disbelief.

"You could try tying him up, but he would just chew through the ropes," Matt added with a smile.

"Ok Mr. Dust, you can go on your way. Go get some coffee and thaw out. Next time have some identification on you."

"Will do, stay safe and thanks for the chat," I said. The police officer rolled up his window shaking his head as he put his car in gear and drove away.

The great part of Earthroaming is regardless of how you describe the previous mentioned *types* of Earthroams, make them your own. That's what a Walk Back, Out and Back, Stay and Play, Rendezvous, Pick Up and Mixed Mode Earthroams are. They are the most common types of Earthroams that I conduct. They were my own designators and before I knew it, they were the terms I was using to describe my adventures to others many years ago and to this very day.

Chapter 8

In the City

"No city should be too large for a man to walk out of in a morning."

Cyril Connolly

The city is a place that for some time I viewed as a distant place that I had a hard time connecting with, however overtime and days spent in some amazing cities around the world I believe it has earned its own chapter. On the grand scale, to me the city is one of overwhelming world that differs greatly that the natural world. However, I do believe people from different walks of life can find the connections to city life in the same way I find connections in the natural, wild and raw parts of the world. If you are that person, The City-roamer, this chapter is for you.

The City Earthroam can be a hard concept to swallow, but you can for sure, without a doubt Earthroam in a city. Just remember the Core Concepts of Earthroaming and you will be ok. Think about it: Nature, which takes the form of the city, provides all. You can still enter with no real plan, know more and carry less, and lead with curiosity. As a matter of fact, I have done some City Earthroaming in Munich, Germany; San Francisco, California; Manila, Philippines; Seattle, Washington; Honolulu, Hawaii; Brisbane, Australia; and Naha, Okinawa, Japan. Earthroaming in a city is very possible and popular. I always say, *grow where you are planted!*

The easiest way to approach this style of Earthroaming is to use a city environment for a Walk Back Earthroam, Out and Back Earthroam, Stay and Play Earthroam, Rendezvous Earthroam and Pick Up Earthroam. All those are different nature-based styles of Earthroams, but simply replace the word *nature* with the word *city* and you can accomplish very similar outcomes. You can go one step further and supplement the Suburban Environment into the City Environment as well because most City Earthroams start in the Suburban Environment. Additionally, you can start your City Earthroam in the city and just go.

A city can be very impactful and influence a different aspect of curiosity. Architecture, museums, food establishments, historical sites, entertainment, social festivals, sporting events, concerts and tourist attractions, to name just a few, can greatly influence curiosity and the decisions of the day. Some of mankind's most interesting accomplishments are held in many cities and can influence curiosity. A city will have pretty much anything you could possibly need for your City Earthroam. Things like food, entertainment, lodging, transportation, communication, medical help and countless opportunities to discover new things. Nature, or in this case the city provides all.

Imagine walking down the street and a flyer promoting your favorite band is stapled to a light pole. You decide to attend the show that evening, and at the same time you catch the aroma of some type of magical food that lights your primal senses to eat on fire. You follow your nose to a hole in the wall restaurant that you decide to dine at, only to hear the couple behind you discussing a small museum that exhibits ancient cultures works of art.

After your meal you hail a cab and make your way to the museum. En route, you call your friend to meet you at the venue later that night, as she loves the same band. You walk meticulously through the exhibits, taking in every clay pot, stone tool, and bone ornament.

During your exploration of the museum, the curator informs you that if you liked this museum, you should visit a local street market a few blocks away that sells items like this and supports local artisans. You make your way to the market and quickly realize you visited this same market ten years ago with your brother before he passed away.

You feel a sense of your brother with you while you walk from booth to booth, smile knowing that the market is still a place he would enjoy today. As you slowly walk away from the market recalling memories of your brother, you discover that you are standing in front of the very venue that your favorite band will be performing at and the show starts in 15 minutes. You link up with your friend who is waiting at the ticket booth, you buy tickets and head inside. After the show you take a cab to the train station to catch the 11:15 light rail to your apartment and call it a day.

I know not everyone will be able to create that same kind of day in my example, but Earthroaming in a city can be amazing. It is what you make of it. Realize that you are not in a remote or rural environment but a city environment, and just make the best of it. Why waste a day when you can experience something new, having no real plan, knowing more and carrying less, and letting curiosity guide you. Just remember the core concepts of Earthroaming and you will connect to your environment in some way. Don't be making hand drill friction fires in New York's Central Park and don't get caught throwing your Atlatl at Edo Castle in Tokyo, Japan, and you should be okay!

One of my best City Earthroams was in Munich, Germany, and was based on a dumb travel mistake. You see, I arrived in Munich almost 48 hours earlier than I was supposed to because I overlooked the time change, flying time differences, and just about everything else. I was going to be teaching at a military installation near a small town called Eschenbach on

Monday starting at 9:00 a.m., however I arrived at the Munich Airport at 7:00 a.m. Saturday morning when I was supposed to arrive Sunday evening at 7:00 pm. As you can see, I had time to kill and curiosity to guide me.

Keep in mind that I know about ten, maybe eleven words in German; please, thank you, beer, North, South, East and West, and I can count to three in German. I figured with my limited German vocabulary, a few free maps I picked up at the airport guest relations booth, a pocket full Euros, and the knowledge that my final destination was over 200 kilometers North of Munich, I should start Earthroaming Norden (German for North).

I left the airport taking a city bus with the destination of a local train station that would start my northern progress to Eschenbach. On this trip, I carried a mid-sized, green, North Face Pack with about one week's worth of clothes (I planned on washing them); simple gear, like a blade, blanket, bottle and no cell phone. My original plan was at the conclusion of the two weeks of training in Eschenbach, I was going to Earthroam in the Czech Republic (which is a stone's throw from Eschenbach Germany) for a bit and then find my way into Austria to do the same.

The bus from the airport dropped me at the train station at just about 8:00 a.m. Now came the challenge to purchase a train ticket.

"Guten morgen," a younger woman in her mid-20s said as I approached the ticket desk.

"Ein...train ticket...Norden Eschenbach bitte," I said with complete confidence in my best German. What I was asking for is, *One train ticket North to Eschenbach please.* The conversation that followed was one that I will never forget.

"One train ticket, North to Eschenbach," the women said behind the counter in perfect English and with a smile on her face.

"You speak English!" I said in complete shock and with a bit of embarrassment. "I am so sorry I do not speak German. Your English is amazing. I am trying my best to learn, but yes... one ticket to Eschenbach. Dankeschon," I said. "Eschenbach is Norden of Munich," I added.

"Yes... I understand. Eschenbach is North of Munich," the young woman said with a side of *I am not an idiot, I speak German.* She paused a moment and then said, "I am not familiar with this place. Please wait one moment." At that point the young women left the counter and consulted with an older gentleman who was typing on a computer sitting at a desk behind her. They spoke back and forth for a minute or two, pointed at a few maps on the table, looked at me, pointed to a computer screen, looked back at the maps, looked back at me, shook their heads and continued talking in German quickly.

"Okay Sir. We have found Eschenbach. Problem. There is no train that will bring you directly there." she said watching my expression.

"That's not a problem," I said.

"You said you wanted to go to Eschenbach, yes?" she said with a bit of confusion.

"Yes. I need to eventually end up in Eschenbach by tomorrow night, but I have very flexible plans," I said.

"That is good, because you will have to take several different trains to arrive in Eschenbach with several hours of time in between," she said.

"Perfect," I said followed by another "dankeschön."

"You are fine with this?" she said with even more confusion over why a person would be fine waiting for several hours between trains.

"I am, and I have no real plans," I said.

"Okay this is good. My colleague is writing down the different trains you will need to take and the wait times in between," she explained.

"Excellent... dankeschön," I said once again. At that moment the gentleman who was sitting behind the woman at the desk brought her a piece of paper with several arrival and departure towns, train numbers, train colors, and train times written on it. She meticulously went over each segment of my journey and watched intently, ensuring I knew where I was going and what I was doing. All together there were seven different segments with plenty of time in between.

"Any questions?" she said with a sense of accomplishment.

"Nein," I said with a smile. She smiled back. "I think I can handle it from here," I said. She nodded in agreement. "Dankeschön, dankeschön, and dankeschön," I said three times as if the first one was not enough.

"Bitte," the young woman said.

I locked eyes with the gentlemen behind her and gave him a "dankeschön."

"Bitte," the gentlemen replied.

I paid for my next train ticket that was leaving in about 30 minutes and was ecstatic for the day ahead. I knew that in between each train, I had several hours of Earthroaming small, local Bavarian towns. Many towns that no tourist or traveler would ever have a reason to stop in or visit. I, however, was going to explore each one and take advantage of the time I had. Each one served as a new destination and an opportunity to lead with curiosity. The next 40 hours were amazing.

I consumed two monster sized pretzels in the first hour, discovered several beer halls with ample amounts of beer, found a monument to a German beer brewer, explored a haunted castle, missed two trains, which resulted in me sleeping in a park under a small arched bridge, was questioned by the *Stadtpolizei* (local police) after trying to hitchhike, consumed more pretzels, convinced a supermarket attendant to give me a ride to the train station after he discovered I was an American from Colorado, drank more beer in small pub (very dodgy), walked some local trails, rode a few more trains, tried schnitzel and eventually walked the remaining way Norden to Eschenbach where I found my small, local hotel and checked in.

"Guten Abend...Dust...checking in," I said.

In perfect English and without missing a beat, "Guten Abend Mr. Dust. Welcome. I am happy to have you here in Eschenbach. How has your day been?" The gentlemen said behind the dark wooden counter.

"Perfect. Just perfect" I said handing the gentlemen my passport and credit card. "Just wunderbar."

Chapter 9

Earthroaming With Others

"Great people are those who make others feel that they, too, can become great."

Mark Twain

When it comes to Earthroaming, you may not always be alone. In all actuality, Earthroaming with others or even a small group can be pretty fulfilling. Yes, the entire Earthroam changes based on the group dynamic and your role within the group dynamic, but Earthroaming with others can lead to amazing experiences.

Group Dynamic Considerations

What is a group? A group is more than two people, who see themselves as a group, who share common goals, and who interact with each other. A role within the group is typically established as soon as the group comes together and establishes the goal/objective/desired end state. In the case of an Earthroam, I have identified six different *roles* that I frequently come across during any type of group Earthroam. Many roles and role theories exist in popular science and literature today. My role designations and descriptions are based on some elements of role theories in science, but are mainly derived from years of guiding, teaching, coaching and mentoring individuals and groups in the outdoors.

Group Role Designators & Descriptions

1. Chief	Leader of group. Sound decision making, employing innovative and creative solutions. Excellent communicator and inspires others with passion, enthusiasm with self-control. Open, firm, fair, calculating, smart, direct, courageous, caring and optimistic.
2. Deputy	Second in command. Non-submissive but accepting of role. Keeps the group on task and organized. Smart, analytical, attune to emotional intelligence, confident, direct, and has an "All for one and one for All" mentality.
3. Companion	Sides with the "chief/deputy." Follow the leader mentality. Encourages or persuade others to adopt power player views. Afraid of being left out. Observant, calculating, self-critical, analytical, and friendly.
4. River	Goes with the flow. Follows group consensus, avoids any group conflict, declares themselves "neutral" or "down for whatever" or "whatever works best." Even-keeled, observant, indecisive, reluctant, and timid.
5. Sharpshooter	Questions ideas (often with aggression), argues, expresses counter points, raises the "what if" question. Pushes back on most group consensus and forces choices to be made. Loud, bold, aggressive,

	assertive and stubborn. Wants to be the Chief.
6. Joker	Breaks tension and can bring group together with humor and point out issues in a comedic sense. Works hard and can fulfill other roles aside from Joker. Often a swing vote in the group. Smart, flexible, funny, innovative, creative, assertive, observant, fresh, analytical, caring and courageous.

The group role designators and descriptions above are consistent in most groups I lead or teach these days. When a group only has three or four people (less than six), people can fulfill multiple roles or shift from one role to another. With groups of six or more, people stick to their roles routinely and rarely shift from one to another. These group role designators and descriptions must be considered when organizing a group Earthroam. How will you fit into the group? What is your role?

When Earthroaming in a group, many amazing, successful and powerful experiences can happen. Groups can create a kinship that clearly isn't of blood relation but still strong and everlasting. Group members take care of each other and do not abandon each other. A division of responsibilities and labors give rise to group accountability and dependability. Deeper connections and understanding of who each group member takes place. A group also provides safety, unity, shared knowledge, shared skills, shared abilities, accomplishment, and reassurance. It is no wonder why people for thousands and thousands of years lived in tribes, clans and groups.

To keep your group on track, unified and motivated consider the following best practices.

1. Know your group, or get to know your group before you start your Earthroam.
2. Address problems and issues quickly. Don't wait and hope they resolve themselves. All they will do is intensify and become major problems.
3. If roles and responsibilities need to be determined and delegated... do it!
4. Break down walls and barriers between group members. Don't let the walls get any higher.
5. Always use non-violent communication.
6. Consider everyone and pay attention. People can and will struggle or hurt. Don't overlook a small indication of a struggle. Include everyone as much as possible.
7. Be honest and forthcoming with information and input.
8. Use active listening when interacting with group members. *Listen* to what someone is saying. Don't just *hear* what they are saying. There is a difference.
9. Conduct activities that makes the group happy and presents a value. Don't prioritize non-relevant or low value activities.
10. Set the right tone of the group Earthroam and manage the group's expectations.

Delegating authorities and determining a leader can be tricky. In an official capacity, If I was guiding a group, I would determine a leader based on some pretty baseline interpersonal skills like communication (verbal and non-verbal), rapport, active listening, physical abilities, social understanding, emotional intelligence and general intelligence. If the group is big enough, let's say six, the group subconsciously will start to determine who the "Chief" is, and all of the following subsequent roles will fall into place. It's a natural process, really. The roles really become defined when uncertainty, problems, and issues are at hand and a decision needs to be made.

Think of the last time you went hiking, in a group, and along your path of travel you came to a split in the trail. Do you go left or right? At that moment, that exact moment a Chief will emerge with a choice or the decision for the group. In this case, the Chief wants to go right. The Sharpshooter challenges the Chief establishing his role as Sharpshooter. The Deputy agrees with the Chief, reinforcing the Chiefs logic for travelling along the right trail. The Joker comes to life as he senses the tension between the newly established Chief and Sharpshooter and tries to lighten the mood. The Companion, sensing the Chief and Deputy have the best argument for traveling along the right path, sides with them. While the River gives a statement of, "I am fine with whatever, but let's make a choice soon, because I am hungry." While this one decision was made, it has established a new group dynamic and these roles will stick until the hike is complete.

Trust Factors in Earthroaming

In almost every group, tribe or clan that has ever existed, trust is a significant factor in group success. Trust is an emotional and logical act. Emotionally, trust is evident when you expose your vulnerabilities to a person or group but believe they will not take advantage of your openness. An example would be informing someone you work with that you have several unpaid speeding tickets, believing they will not inform your supervisor of your speeding ticket problem in order to prevent your progression in the company.

Logically, trust is present when you have assessed the probabilities of gain or loss, calculated expected utility based on performance history, and concluded that the person in question will behave in a predictable manner. An example of this is my kids believe that when I drop them off at school, I will also pick them up. This is an expected outcome based on my previous performance history of picking them up on-time at school. If I forgot to pick them up one day, this would be a breakdown in trust.

In practice, trust is both emotional and logical. I trust you because I have experienced and seen your trustworthiness and because I have faith in you. Below are the four most common dimensions of trust.

Predictability. To be constantly forecasting ahead is a normal part of the human condition. We build internal models of the world based on our experiences and what others tell us, and then use these models to guess what will and can happen next. We can assess and prepare for threats and make plans to achieve our objectives.

Value Exchange. Most of what we do with other people is based around value exchange. Simple relationships are built form value exchange. Value exchange is the exchange of goods—I will swap you two pigs for one sheep. It is easy to calculate the value in such material bargaining. Things get more complex when less tangible forces come into play. Taxpayers pay police officers' salaries in exchange for protection and security.

Delayed Reciprocity. Exchange is not just about an immediate swapping of sheep and cows. What makes groups and societies really work is that something is given now, but the return is paid back some time in the future. Think of a credit card or automobile loan. The advantage of this is that we can create a more flexible environment, where you can get what you need when you need it.

Exposed Vulnerabilities. When we trust other people, we may not only be giving them something in hope of getting something else back in the future, we may also be exposing ourselves in a way that makes it easy to be taken advantage of. If I purchase a car from you and I lack knowledge of cars, you can lie to me about the condition of the car, so you get a better bargain. If I tell you in confidence about the problems I am having with my finances and need money, you could use this to obtain a goal within your own personal agenda, like getting me to sell my vintage sports car at a lower price because you envy it.

How do the dimensions of trust tie into a Group Earthroam? Is one dimension of trust more prevalent than the others? During a Group Earthroam people need to demonstrate behaviors that build trust. Let's take the Four Dimensions of Trust: delayed reciprocity, predictability, exposed vulnerabilities, and value exchange, and apply them to a Group Earthroam Scenario.

If I am Earthroaming in a group of four people and they all fail at catching fish, but I catch four fish and give everyone in the group a fish to eat, I would expect:

1. Through the Trust Dimension of Delayed Reciprocity, on a later date, I would be repaid a fish or given a fish to eat when I have caught none.
2. Through the Trust Dimension of Predictability, based on similar and previous scenarios involving the catching of fish, that the group would pay me back a fish
3. Through the Trust Dimension of Exposed Vulnerabilities, I would know that the other members of the group told me they were horrible at fishing and hunting. I would not use this information to further advance myself in the group or use it as a tool to manipulate outcomes.
4. Through the Trust Dimension of Value Exchange, the members of the group returned the value of the fish by trapping a rabbit and collecting wild mushrooms to eat.

The Four Trust Dimensions are important on a Group Earthroam as well as all daily activities. You can see how a breakdown or loss of trust can greatly impact the outcomes of a Group Earthroam. If trust is broken or damaged, here are some behaviors that build and rebuild trust.

1. Be honest, tell the truth, and talk straight.
2. Genuinely care for others. Show you care by being respectful.
3. Be open and authentic.
4. Say you're sorry. Make things right when you are wrong.
5. Don't bad mouth others in the group.
6. Be loyal to the group.
7. Make things happen and deliver results.
8. Continuously improve and get better at your mistakes. Increase your capabilities.
9. Address issues head on... even the uncomfortable ones.
10. Include everyone and never isolate anyone.
11. Never assume you have all the answers.
12. Manage expectations.
13. Listen before you speak.
14. Say what you mean and mean what you say.
15. Extend trust to those who have earned your trust.

When Earthroaming with others, many human factors must be considered and continuously valuated. Group roles are not always set in stone and can alter through different environments nd activities specific to the Earthroam. Sometimes comfort levels can change along with the nvironment, and those changing confidence levels and insecurities can impact their group role. ust remember that all relationships are based on trust, and during an Earthroam, trust is ssential. No matter what, trust is the most important factor in all groups. Trust is the building lock of a tribe, and the lack thereof leads to the destruction of a tribe, as well.

Chapter 10

Safety Considerations

"For safety is not a gadget but a state of mind."

Eleanor Everet

Earthroaming is inherently dangerous in many ways. The opportunity to encounter dangers like wild animals, poisonous plants, health issues, and extreme weather can occur daily and even hourly. One of the reasons why we Earthroam is to have a real situation where survival, bushcraft, primitive living and wilderness self-reliance skills can be applied. When put ourselves in less than ideal situations, the likelihood of sickness, injuries or even death increases.

When it comes to Earthroaming, some dangers can't always be mitigated or prevented. Or can they? Do we have the ability to mitigate most of the dangers and hazards associated with Earthroaming? Looking back, have you ever said these phrases to yourself: *I had this feeling,* or *I told myself three times to…* or *I knew I should have…* and completely ignored them? That's called intuition and it is typically correct. Let's list some common dangers and hazards and see how we could have mitigated the danger.

1. Predator animal encounter
2. Lightning strike

3. Poisonous plant
4. Dehydration
5. Flash flood
6. Snake bite
7. Knife wound
8. Frostbite
9. Slip and fall
10. Rockslide

I am sure as you read the ten dangers, you were probably thinking of ways to mitigate the risks right off the bat. To avoid a snake bite, you don't pick up a snake (obviously), watch where you step, look before you pick something up, and the list goes on. That is called acknowledgment of threat. When we acknowledge that threats exist in all environments, we are taking the first step to mitigate them. If we disregard them or completely just ignore them altogether, we will not be able to prevent them. When we acknowledge that threats exist and that we are all susceptible to them, we can establish the Pattern of Life in any environment and attempt to mitigate them.

The Pattern of Life is the routine patterns of an environment; like the individual sounds that exist, the smells that move through the air, air pressure, winds, and temperatures. All environments have a pattern of life, we have a Pattern of Life. People have the unique ability to tell when something is wrong internally or externally with their body. Our Pattern of Life is an amazing adaptation to give us indications and warnings of "problems" in our bodies. Think of lack of sweat is a sign of dehydration, a rise in temperature is our bodies way to kill viruses and even us sneezing is our body's attempt to expel foreign bodies from our system. Every person and every environment has a pattern of life.

When we can consciously and subconsciously observe, feel, and integrate into an environment's Pattern of Life, we can mitigate many risks. We will be able to see the warning signs of progressive or sudden changes and take appropriate actions. I am sure we have all been in a natural environment, fully immersed, when we hear singing birds change their tune to one of alarm. Or maybe you have been out on a hike and a hard burst of wind with cool temperatures hits you, a sign a storm is following closely behind. These examples are a disruption in the normal Pattern of Life. Even a city can have a Pattern of Life that many people can understand. The seasons can and will impact an environment's Pattern of Life, but a pattern still exists.

A ***Keyhole*** is when we ignore or deny ourselves the ability to fully immerse into a Pattern of Life. We become so focused on a task we cannot see outside of the keyhole. We only have one vantage point and that is the one directly in front of us. We become focused on one point of view, one task, one goal, and we lose the immersion into the Pattern of Life. I use the term Keyhole often with students when they are learning the KSA of primitive trapping because I watch them become so focused on building and setting traps, that they miss the opportunity to take a rabbit or squirrel a few feet away with a rabbit stick. The worst Keyholes are when people use knives. New and experienced Earthroamers will be working a piece of wood with a knife and Keyhole on the knife, forgetting their leg or fingers in relation to the blade. With one swoosh of the knife, an entire new set of bloody problems has just surfaced.

The terms Acknowledgement of Threat, Pattern of Life and Keyhole are all terms that deal directly with Situational Awareness. The essential, the must-have for every Earthroamer is Situational Awareness. This is the one tool that can help an Earthroamer mitigate risk and avoid seriously dangerous or life-threatening issues. An Earthroamer should have amazing situational awareness, and the best ways to have situational awareness is acknowledge threats exist, immerse yourself in the pattern of life, and avoid keyholes. As earthroamers, we must stay aware, we must be aware and listen to our intuition.

Chapter 11

Know Your Enemies

"We often give our enemies the means for our own destruction."

Aesop

Earthroaming Enemies are the physical, mental, emotional, and primal stresses that a person or group can encounter on an Earthroam. Earthroaming enemies have the ability to take an already difficult day and make it worse. However, your ability to cope with them and overcome them will ultimately lead to an amazing Earthroaming experience. On every single Earthroam, I've had to face down at least one Earthroaming Enemy. They are always around and can take over at a moment's notice. At the end of this chapter, I will show you how to battle and overcome the Earthroaming Enemies.

Loneliness is a major enemy of Earthroaming. Being isolated in areas of the world that are harsh and extreme can create a sense of loneliness. Loneliness can lead to feelings of extreme hopelessness and despair. We are all human and need human contact through various means that can break the loneliness grip on our mind. We must be prepared to handle loneliness when Earthroaming.

Boredom plays a role in Earthroaming Enemies. Many people who Earthroam are self-guided and have very easy ways to overcome boredom, while on the flip side of the coin, some eople lack the self-initiated actions to deal with boredom and overcome it. Boredom comes rom a few different sources: repetitiveness, lack of personal interest, and mental fatigue. Boredom can cause bouts of depression, frustration, and anxiety. I can attest that boredom is omething I have to overcome often. I aim to obtain a sense of flow or complete mental mmersion in a task to overcome boredom. Boredom can and will be a pretty constant Earthroaming Enemy.

Fatigue is also pretty common. We have all experienced fatigue from any number of vents in our lives, like lack of sleep, energy exertion, improper hydration, poor diet, withdrawals from an addiction (caffeine, nicotine, sugar, etc.), and too much rest. During an Earthroam, you will be fatigued without a doubt. Understand that when a person is fatigued your nental ability is reduced and this can become dangerous to you and others in your group. People ave the ability to summon enough focus, energy and drive to overcome fatigue for periods of ime, but this will eventually lead to a *fatigue crash*. In Earthroaming, this could lead to loss of ife and limb.

Uncertainty is a significant Earthroaming Enemy. Remember that Earthroaming lacks a olid or guiding plan. This lack of planning causes uncertainty. While uncertainty is, in many ways, a desired state of being for many who Earthroam, it can also lead to doubt, hopelessness, anic, fear, anxiety, and depression. People panic when they have to think about sourcing their wn water, food, and shelter. The uncertainty of not knowing when the next drink of water, neal, or place to sleep causes many people to stay out of the wilds of the world where certainty s a constant.

Hunger will certainly be an Earthroaming Enemy. Hunger can affect motivations, ttitudes, morale, and your ability to carry on Earthroaming. We have all been hungry or witnessed someone who is hungry and can attest to the complete change in their motivations and attitudes. I believe the term today is *Hangry*. This is not the first time this book has touched on food or hunger from lack of food. It is a huge factor and must be considered and mitigated when Earthroaming.

Thirst is a life taker. Thirst is the first step to becoming dehydrated. It is our bodies innate way to tell us we need to drink. Drink water when you have the supply. Our body can hold far more water and carry it then our backs and hands. When you are thirsty, you must listen to what your body is telling you... Drink! When we are thirsty, our senses can become dull or not as attuned to the surrounding environment. This dulling of senses can lead to injury, or in extreme cases, even death.

Pain is our body telling our mind that something is wrong. While Earthroaming pain will come in many forms. The actual pain is not harmful but can lead to discomfort and future problems. Pain is a natural response but can be blocked or tolerated through intense focused concentration on a task. All people have a pain tolerance, but pain tolerance does not mean the issue is not gone. Pain can and will produce a significant emotional, mental, and physical problem when Earthroaming if it is not reduced or eliminated.

Heat and Cold require necessary actions to increase or decrease, and both can be life taking if not properly mitigated. The extremes of both are factors that, when not addressed, can lead to serious physical and mental problems. Both can impact your ability to think, your motivations, morale, and your overall focus and accomplishment of a task. If your body is overheating, cooling temperatures can reduce the overheating. When your body is losing heat, making a fire and creating heat to treat external bodily elements (fingers, toes, nose, legs, arms, etc.) allows the internal bodily elements (brain, liver, lungs, heart, etc.) to continue to function with efficiency.

Knowledge, Skills and Abilities, or the lack thereof, are a huge Earthroaming Enemy. When we lack knowledge, this can impact our skills and abilities. We can have knowledge but lack the ability to execute the skills. All three work hand and hand. We need KSAs to battle the previous mentioned enemies of Earthroaming. If I lack the KSA to get food, identify clean water, or increase the temperature to stay warm, I am creating an Earthroaming Enemy from a lack of KSA. This is a significant problem. A lack of KSA can directly cause loss of life and limb.

Two ways to overcome the Earthroaming Enemies are acknowledging your own *self-deception* and determining our own *self-reliance.* Both are very much real and can prevent the loss of life or serious energy. However, both require the other to be effective to the Earthroamer. Self-deception is when we lie to ourselves about… well, just about anything. We can deceive ourselves about our physical abilities, or skills in the outdoors, and levels of knowledge regarding a specific subject. We literally lie to ourselves subconsciously, and then we believe it. The best part about it is that on some level, we know we are lying to ourselves. We do this all the time. We tell ourselves we can do something when we know deep down that we really can't.

Self-reliance can have many meanings and is often used as a catch-all term in many outdoor circles, but true self-reliance is your reliance on your own KSA and not that of others. Self-reliance in reference to Earthroaming has two origins. One origin is derived from the writings of Ralph Waldo Emerson, who said follow your own path, do not blindly follow others, blaze your own path and establish your own culture. The second origins are of my own; self-reliance begins when we acknowledge our self-deception, allowing us to know ourselves and seek self-improvement. Ultimately, through our acknowledgment of our self-deceptions we can overcome and build into our self-reliance.

Why do we self-deceive? To appear better than we are. To display a level of competency that isn't there. To display more heroism in a situation or in daily life than we really have. To come off as more friendly than we actually are. To present more intelligence than we really have. The heart of the matter is perhaps the idea that you are hiding something or keeping the truth from yourself. There could be something we don't like about ourselves and, rather than acknowledge it, knowing yourself and confronting it, we would rather ignore it and move onto nicer things that are easier to accept, things that make us feel good.

To battle the enemies of earthroaming we, you, I need to stop lying to ourselves. We need to ask ourselves, *"What am I lying about, or what am I hiding from?"* Stop self-deceiving. It is dangerous and can take your life in a variety of ways. If we lack the KSA in a subject, that's alright. Educate yourself and learn more about it. Know yourself and seek self-improvement. I don't know everything there is to know about everything. There will come a moment when we are asked or required to *do* something and we know we cannot, but we lie to ourselves and say we can. This is an attempt to hide our actions from closer scrutiny. At times we are displeased by something we say or do and routinely make every attempt to hide this as best we can. In Earthroaming, deceiving yourself in your KSA can get yourself killed or others killed or seriously injured.

Sometimes, the hardest step is to acknowledge that what we think we know, we don't. What we believe ourselves to be able to do, we can't. We lack the KSA to overcome them. And our self-deception can have a wide impact. We can deceive ourselves and then consciously or subconsciously deceive others about our KSA, attitudes, personality, intelligence and honesty.

There can be a second and third order effect, as our self-deception can impact many people in our lives and sphere of influence. Although it can be hard to admit this, the acknowledgment is truly the first step in self-reliance.

If we take the ideas of Ralph Waldo Emerson, like not blindly following others, following our own paths, knowing yourself, and seeking self-improvement, we can overcome the Enemies of Earthroaming. If I know I need to work on my physical fitness, but I tell myself I am ok or I can get by, I have just self-deceived. If I cognitively acknowledge my own self-deception and seek self-improvement, I will not only improve my body, but I will build my self-reliance. If I hide my real capabilities of fire making to myself (self-deception), but acknowledge my shortfalls or deceptive cover ups on an aspect of fire making I don't know well (hand drill friction fire), I have now found my point of deception and my self-reliance KSA to improve on.

If we never self-deceived we would never know what we need to work on to build our self-reliance. No better example of self-deception comes to mind than the time I was rafting a section of the Arkansas River near Buena Vista Colorado in some serious Class IV-V rapids on an inflatable, sit-on-top kayak with a cracked paddle blade and a poorly sized PFD (personal floatation device). I entered in an Extreme Adventure Race that encompassed a 15 mile run, 50 mile mountain bike, 15 mile paddle on the Arkansas River, land navigation to 20 different points with miles spread between points, a couple Tyrolean traverses across canyons, rock scrambling, and just about anything else the race creators wanted to put in our way. I was a solo racer because I could never find anyone to race with me or make a team. So it goes!

After completing the first section of the 15 mile run I was to meet my support crew at a racer's put-in location along the Arkansas River, where we would load up on our kayaks and take off to continue the race. It was late spring and the snowpack from the snowfall was huge, resulting in a monster-sized melt that swelled the rivers and streams and created some amazing and deadly rapids.

As I approached the river's edge, I could see my crew standing and encouraging me to go on.

"You got this... there are only like four or five people in front of you. You can catch them on the river!" my crew said with complete encouragement.

"I feel good. I think I can pull this off. Let me get some more water," I said as I squeezed a bottle made up of half water and half electrolyte mix into my mouth. As I got closer to the water's edge, I could hear the roar, the pure rage of the white water ripping its way along the Arkansas River. I could see nothing but white water and chaos on the river.

"Alright racer, let me give you your river brief," A voice said from behind me. An older gentleman, about mid-50s, was working the rafting put-in location and he was to give each racer their river brief before taking off. "Serious big water today. I have not seen it like this for some time."

"Awesome," I said with a bit of nervousness growing inside.

"Since the river is so intense, you have the option to omit this section of the race and a 60 minute penalty will be added to your total race time. I believe you are the sixth racer so far and only one racer before you has executed the river section, and I believe he was a collegiate rower or Olympic paddler, or something like that," he said.

"Ok... that's interesting. So, a bit of a challenge, it sounds like?" I said.

"More like suicide," he said with a chuckle. "We have no one to assist you on the river if you are to flip and tip. It is all self-rescue. I will say it again. We have no stationary aids along he river to help you. All I can say is if you flip, keep your toes up, and make every effort to get o the edge. Walk to the road and thumb a ride back into town," he said with all seriousness.

"Holy shit. This is pretty intense," I said looking at my crew. At this same time, a team of hree arrived and were given the same brief. Without hesitation, they took the 60-minute penalty. was extremely nervous at this point.

"Do you think you can do it?" one of my crew asked. "I think you can crush this."

I have paddled all around the world and run some pretty amazing rapids. I spent some ime on the Tully River and the Barron River in Australia, sections of the Colorado River, ections of the Arkansas River, The Youghiogheny River in Pennsylvania, and countless others round the US. Hell, I spent hours and days kayaking along the South China Sea during some retty treacherous situations in the pursuit of monster trophy fish, but I had never seen the water he way it was that day. That day, the river was uncontrollable rage. Pure hate and discontent for nyone that chooses to ride her rapids. Potential suicide for the unskilled or untrained.

"Let's do it" I said.

"It's on you man," the older gentlemen said. "I have lived along this river for 30 years, nd every so often this volume of water comes our way. Good luck, and again, you assume all isk... self-rescue and swim hard for the river's edge."

"No worries. I got this."

"You are a crazy Donny, but you have this," my crew said as one of them handed me my FD.

I am going to be honest. I was scared. I was feeling fear, intense fear, but I kept telling nyself that I can do this. Not the same, *I can do it attitude* you might tell yourself when you are ired after a long hike and have to walk a little bit further to your car. This was more of an *if you don't do it, you will die of embarrassment* feeling. The same list of rivers and rafting experiences I detailed above are the same justifications I used to deceive myself into thinking I was a professional paddler. I had not paddled in any big water for well over ten years and I did not train for this level of rapid. However, I told myself that I could, when I should have said *It's only a 60-minute penalty.* Completely dumb! I would have no one but myself to rescue me. I would be swimming against thousands of cubic feet of water, all rushing down on me at once, negotiating countless trees and branches waiting to impale me, there would be countless seen and unseen boulders waiting to smash into me, and the freezing cold temps required a wetsuit to battle.

"I got this" I said again with a breath of deception. I grabbed my inflatable kayak and busted paddle and set-in in the only ten feet of semi-calm water that existed. I buckled my helmet and said, "See you all at the pull-out location... wish me luck."

The older gentleman walked over as I sat on the water's edge atop an inflatable kayak with a broken paddle taped together and said, "Stay to the right along the river. There are several forks, you must take every right fork to stay clear of the debris along the run. Also, don't miss the pull out or you are running the entire river all the way to Salida. Look for the blue flags."

"Gotcha, self-rescue, stay to the right, blue flags…" I said as my body began to shiver from the lack of movement and the freezing cold water that was already destroying my morale.

"Good luck," he said.

At this point I pushed off from the bank and was completely consumed by the river. Still atop my inflatable kayak, I positioned myself in most advantageous areas that my paddle, kayak and body could get to. The rapids were so intense and grand in size that my kayak would bend in half when hitting them. My body shivered from the cold, but my senses were on fire knowing that death could be a few paddles away. I stuck to the right forks per the older gentleman's guidance but found myself being pulled to the left fork like a fish on a hook on several occasions. I had to battle downed trees and massive whitewater that engulfed huge boulders stretched across the river like a set of fence posts.

I picked my runs, path, and sections of the river carefully as best I could, but at other times I was told by the river where I was going. Then, in what seemed like hours of battling the river, I saw blue flags and knew I was close to safety. I could not overshoot the pull out or it was many more miles to the next feasible pull out location. As I approached, I could barely find my crew among a sea of spectators and race officials watching my quick approach. I kept my focus and aimed my kayak to the small pull-out spot like I had done a thousand times before. Before I knew it, I quickly found myself back on solid ground with high-fives and thumbs up from people watching.

"Holy cow! We were so scared!" my crewmember said as she tossed me a towel.

"That has to be one of the dumbest things I have ever done in my life," I said, with complete amazement that I was alive. "Never again will I listen to myself and not listen to myself at the same time," I declared.

When all was said and done, out of 245 racers, I finished in 7th place overall. According to one race official, 45 racers attempted the river; 20 completed the river, while 25 hitchhiked or were picked up along the side of the road after swimming to the river's edge. Six kayaks/rafts were lost to the river, never to be found again. Nobody died, thank goodness, but 10 were treated for or showed initial signs of hypothermia.

Bottomline, to overcome the Enemies of Earthroaming you have to stop the self-deceptions and acknowledge when you're overstepping your KSA. Take the focus of your deception and build the KSA around it. This will increase your true self-reliance on an

Earthroam and maybe save your life if you ever come face to face with some big water rapids on an inflatable kayak. I was nothing but lucky that day.

Chapter 12

Let's Give Something Back

"It is every man's obligation to put back into the world at least the equivalent of what he takes out of it."

Albert Einstein

The most important aspect of Earthroaming is giving back. I always give back to the land that I take from. I ensure that the people who Earthroam with me give back as well. It is my responsibility to the land and my responsibilities to my children's children's children to have a place to Earthroam. It is the responsibility of every Earthroamer to do their part and give back. I feel guilty at times if I have to cut the branches of tree to build a shelter. I feel bad when I must fell a tree to make a strong and solid ridge pole. However, I overcome that guilt and know that nature has provided that resource for me and I will return the gift. How I do this is comes in a couple of different forms that I hope everyone can start doing.

Directly Give Back is when I plant trees and all manner of plants organic to the environment. This could come in the form of transplanting trees to more favorable locations to grow or planting the seeds of different trees in areas that are barren or need new growth. I disperse wildflower seeds in areas that are vacant of color, offering new food sources and opportunities for biodiversity. No matter what I plant or transplant, I make sure it is native and organic to the natural environment and does not compete or conflict with native species.

Pack Out Trash. This is a no brainer, but I still know it needs to be said. If you see trash, pick it up and pack it out. It's our job to do it as Earthroamers. If it is your trash, pack it out with you. To be honest when I come across trash, I find a way to use it to my advantage; if I find a plastic bottle, I can carry water in it and use it as a split lashing. Potato chip bags make excellent folded fishing lures, old cans are turned into arrow points, glass bottles or broken glass... hell, that is a flintknappers dream to turn some broken glass bottles into a few arrowheads when on an Earthroam.

Just do your part and pack out your trash and any other trash you may come across. Look, nobody is going to give you an award, nobody is going to know that you did your part and packed out somebody else's trash. Do it because it is the right thing to do. Having discipline and courage means doing the right thing when nobody's looking.

Never Take the First Shot. That's right, I never take the first shot. What that means is if I have rabbit, deer, squirrel, turkey, grouse, dove, raccoon, or even elk dead in my sites and I know I could take it... I let it go. For me, that is a way of giving back to the land. I know for some that seems crazy, especially if you have not eaten in a day or two. It is, but I feel great about it and know the land does to.

I get a sense of nourishment from giving back in this way. Many times, I have had elk ranged and sighted with my bow and I let it go. Even when I am fishing, the first fish I catch I give back to the water. It’s the right thing to do. Even if I build ten deadfall traps and set them along a nice rocky area, I know I will yield some game, and I set one off as a way to not only take, but to give, too.

As an Earthroamer, never taking the first shot feels right. It is something very deep and meaningful to me. In 2016, I had a female elk tag that I was looking to fill while on an Earthroam. I was doing an Out and Back Earthroam and knew my chances were high for an elk, as I was seeing all kinds of tracks and signs along my path. Despite the signs, I had not seen any actual elk that I could target. I had found hour-old scat, bed-down locations, and some frequented trails that I know were part of a pattern of life for the elk in the area, and I knew it was only a matter of time. In this area I could even hear big bull elk screaming in the distance and knew the area I was in was full of opportunities. I decided to make a quick grass and leaf bed for the night and wake up early to catch this herd during its morning movements. I did just that.

It's important to add I don't hunt with any rifles or compound bows. All my hunting is by way of archery. All arrows are homemade, all bows are homemade, and hunting points are in accordance with the states hunting rules and regulations (stone or steel). I am typically barefoot or in moccasins, I never wear camouflage, and I never cover myself in some type of animal urine. Not my thing or style. If it's your style, you do you! Nothing wrong with that.

I woke early from my sasquatch sleeping bag and was on the hunt. Life becomes easy when you sleep in what you hunt in. Anyway, I was able to lock into a small group of cow elk and was playing the wind nicely, keeping my scent from crossing their noses. The sun was just starting to light up the eastern horizon and I knew I still had some low light screening to play into my actions. I was moving barefoot, slowly, to a slightly elevated position with a clear line of site on a small trail that was going to be full of morning traffic any minute. I scouted this the day before and knew this trail was a major thoroughfare and was going to yield the results I was looking for.

Sure enough, after about a 15 minute approach to my firing location, and another five minutes waiting, I could see four cow elk meandering towards my location, all of which offered a perfect flanking shot if they stayed in their direction of travel. I am an instinctive shooter, so I don't draw an arrow back and hold it in position while aiming and then fire. No, I have fired hundreds upon thousands of arrows and know when I draw back and release exactly where the arrow will hit. This requires a quick pull and release, letting my instincts (from shooting countless arrows at different distances) take over the shot and *feeling* the arrow to the target.

All four of the cow elk closed the distance, moving toward me without awareness of my presence. I had an arrow knocked and was ready. They continued their approach with a few yards of dispersion between them. I slowly elevated my bow in preparation to shoot, knowing I was going to let the first cow elk go by as this was my opportunity to give back. I did just that. The first cow elk was well within range at 15 yards and I knew the others would follow her path and present the same range. I sat motionless, arrow nocked and ready to fire, when a funny thing happened. The first cow elk stopped directly in front of me and lowered her head to munch on some grass and scrub while the other three stopped and went back from the direction they came. No alarm was given, and I provided no threats in the air. The other three conducted a military about-face and marched away.

Now my moral conundrum was in full swing. I knew that if I shot this cow elk, I would be taking what I had already given back. It was a truly challenging situation. This cow elk was offering a perfect flank shot and I knew without a shadow of a doubt I could take her; however, she was my give-back. I hoped that the other three would return and that it would all work out, but they never did. About five minutes after the other cow elk left, the one standing directly in front of me turned to make her way in the direction of the other three.

As she began to leave, two tiny elk calves appeared out of nowhere next to her and followed her without a care in the world. I was shocked. I was in complete disbelief that I missed them. It was like a Las Vegas magic trick, suddenly seeing two tiny elk appear out of nowhere. Maybe it was the low light at this point, the tall grass, my sleep, my complete focus on their mother and her friends—who knows, but I am thankful still to this day that I gave back and didn't take the cow elk. I am glad I did the right thing when nobody was looking. I would have felt horrible if I took that mother elk and left her babies on their own. I understand how nature and life in the wild works, probably more than most people, but on that day, I was able to give back something that many people might not be able to give back. For me, on that day, it was life.

We as a species take so much from this land and offer little in return. We need to make every effort to make this world better and more natural for our health and the planet's health. Find a way to give that fits your pattern of life. Maybe a donation, a community cleanup, or just taking care of the wild lands that Earthroamers find peace and connection in. Every effort, no matter how small and unnoticed counts. Let's give back together!

Chapter 13

Let's Put It All Together

"Great things are done by a series of small things brought together."

Vincent Van Gogh

I think Van Gogh said it best: *Great things are done by a series of small things brought together.* Earthroaming in the big picture might seem overwhelming and a bit extreme, but make it your own and just go. Start small and focus on your approach to better understand the core concepts of Earthroaming: lead with curiosity, know more while carrying less, have no plan, and nature provides all. If you stick to those concepts, you can't go wrong.

On your next day hike, truly let curiosity guide you. Maybe you'll see a new animal track crossing the trail, a strange tree standing on a hill, or a bird circling in the distance, and that could all lead to amazing discoveries and new experiences because you were curious enough to follow them. Even if a discovery has already been found, to you, or maybe even your group, it could be brand new. Just because something has been found by somebody else for the first time, doesn't mean it won't be just as amazing to you when you discover it for the first time.

Nature will provide all that you need. Don't forget that. She has been giving nonstop for millions of years to the lives she has created and supported. She has not failed us, and we must remember not to fail her. Allow yourself to create with her and your Earthroaming experiences will be amazing and memorable.

Drop the plan. That is the point really—get outside and just be. I believe and know the idea of Earthroaming can be life-changing for any person, but it starts with you. Break free from what you have been told an outdoor experience is and just Earthroam. Earthroaming is not about telling you *what* to think, but *how* to think. Freedom in the wilds of the world awaits when Earthroaming.

Never let gear replace your knowledge, skills and abilities. Knowing more and carrying less will not only save you money in the long term, but it will give you complete freedom from the stuff that weighs down your pack. When people tell you that *you must have this,* or *this is a necessity,* don't believe them. You can do so much more on an Earthroam when you have nothing. I tell myself that when I Earthroam, the objective is to walk into the wilds of the world with nothing and walk out with everything. That is what my objective is, and I meet that objective every time.

To start Earthroaming, ensure you have the KSA to do so. If you lack the KSA, leverage experts who do. It will take time, but we all start somewhere. Be wary of those who can only tell you knowledge and can't demonstrate the skills because of a lack of ability. If someone wants to educate you on the KSA of survival, bushcraft, primitive and wilderness self-reliance and they are out of shape, careless, and told you there is only *ONE WAY AND NO OTHER WAY*...run! They probably couldn't catch you anyway.

You must be mentally, physically, emotionally, and primal strong to Earthroam. I recommend starting your first Earthroaming trips in groups. Establish a group of Roamers in your local area who are like-minded, who each bring value to an Earthroam. Give your group a cool name and start Earthroaming on a regular basis. Learn from your fellow Roamers and respect each other as you Earthroam together. Hell, if you want to meet every Wednesday night to discuss Earthroaming KSA, the core concepts, and loosely plan future Earthroams... go for it! Remember to make it your own.

You must have the physical abilities to Earthroam. Some skills are innate, and some, like physical abilities, are built upon with great time and effort. You may have the skills to swim fast, but your ability to swim fast comes from possessing strong arms, back, and leg muscles, which you may develop with regular training, proper diet, and exercise. That's the truth. Earthroaming requires more than just picking up a knife and heading into the backcountry to perform a skill. The question is this: can you take that skill and not just do it for the hell of it, but truly live from it?

Proper diet, exercise, and training will enhance your abilities over time and with routine dedication. Becoming healthy will never hurt! A few concepts I apply to enable and enhance my mental, physical, emotional, and primal abilities are: eating wild foods, performing functional fitness routines, sleeping when I am tired, fasting, using different types of meditation, forest bathing, having as much sex as possible, creating *things* all the time, socializing, and Earthroaming.

Lastly, to start Earthroaming you must have the desire to do it. You have to have that inner fire and drive to live life and experience the world like so few have done before. That is hard to do, but completely possible. That's why I stopped Earthroaming for a time to write this book to share what I have learned, so that you and others like you can start to experience the world the way I have and will for many years to come. To start down the pathway of Earthroaming and becoming n Earthroamer, follow the Earthroaming core concepts when you are in the woods, deserts, ungles, mountains, wetlands, and cities of the world. And they are:

1. Curiosity lead
2. Knowing more while carrying less,
3. Not having a plan
4. Nature provides all

3uild your KSA of Earthroaming focused on:

1. Creativity
2. Fire
3. Water
4. Food
5. Shelter
6. Navigation
7. Camp Craft
8. Fitness Abilities

stablish a Tribe of Earthroamers that are:

1. Like Minded
2. Bring a Value to the Tribe
3. Promote Learning
4. Are Respectful of Everyone

Increase your mental, physical, emotional and primal abilities through:

1. Eating wild foods
2. Performing functional fitness routines
3. Sleep when tired
4. Fasting
5. Meditation
6. Forest Bathing
7. Have Sex
8. Create all the time
9. Socialize
10. Earthroam

Hands down, the most important step in Earthroaming and becoming an Earthroamer is to want it and then do it!

If you want to take all your survival, bushcraft, primitive and wilderness self-reliance skills and actually use them for a real living experience, then Earthroaming is for you. If you want to walk the landscapes of the world the same way our ancestors did, then Earthroaming is for you. If you want to gain a deep appreciation for the world and people around you, then Earthroaming is for you. If you are tired of having to live by strict rules and want the autonomy to learn something new and then make it your own, then Earthroaming is for you! Want it and then do it!

Conclusion

In the End

"The best endings resonate because they echo a word, phrase, or image from earlier in the story, and the reader is prompted to think back to that reference and speculate on a deeper meaning."

James Plath

I was 14 years old when I picked up a 1986 Army Survival FM (Field Manual) from a flea market in Lakewood New Jersey. As I flipped through the pages of the FM, I saw photos and examples of different survival methods like edible plants, traps, and survival shelter concepts that I had been exploring as a child and doing as a young teen. I was never formally taught survival, bushcraft, primitive, or wilderness self-reliance skills when I was a child or even as a teen. I was just curious, creative, and loved being outside. My classroom was always in the woods and wetlands and the places in between. Curiosity was my faithful teacher that never had a substitute and creativity was my lesson, homework, and test.

I didn't know the significance of that book then, but I now know it was a huge factor in my life moving forward. It was the textbook that brought all the ideas and tried failures as a child into fruition as a teen. It provided clarity to unanswered questions and a path to move forward. That Army FM was the spark that lit the fire for exploring the world with complete freedom. It shaped my concept of Earthroaming and me into an Earthroamer.

EARTHROAMER

I never will classify myself as a survivalist, bushcrafter, primitive technologist, or wilderness self-reliance-ist. I teach all those skills and I love, and I mean *love*, doing it. I don't *do* survival, however. I don't *do* bushcraft, I just don't *do* primitive skills; I Earthroam. A term that encompasses survival, bushcraft, primitive skills, and wilderness self-reliance in many ways that are unique to me and now, hopefully unique to you. Hell, I can't even call myself a hunter, backpacker, hiker, skier climber, snowshoer, archer, or even mountaineer. I find a love and passion in all of them, and Earthroaming is in all of them.

I will be honest. To walk through the wilds of the world with no plan, knowing more while carrying less, utilizing everything from nature, and letting curiosity guide you takes a kind of knowledge, skills, and abilities you can't learn if you don't do. You have to *do it.* In all reality, it takes a certain type of crazy as well, but the rewards are endless and worthwhile. Earthroaming is an opportunity to experience the world in the same way that our early ancestors experienced it and the way a handful of people still do across the world. Earthroaming will always be my platform to experience the world and all it has to offer.

In the end we are all the same. We may try to separate ourselves into rank, files, and columns, but we are all people of the Earth. We are all bonded through our creativity and curiosity, and our endless, innate desire to roam this planet. We are all able to roam this beautiful planet because it is what we are called to do. That is what Earthroaming is about: letting our curiosity guide us and discovering what is new. I live by the saying, *a way, not the way,* but I always answer the innate and natural call of Earthroaming, because I truly believe it is *the* way.

Donny Dust is a Marine Corps Veteran of 12 years of service with an honorable discharge in 2011. Donny is a worldwide expert in remote primitive survival, emergency preparedness and ancient/historical technologies. Donny has taken his time in service and days living among the wild landscapes of the world to offer his one of a kind presentations on resiliency, leadership, experimental archeology and communication. Donny is the author of the hit book *Scavenger*, has worked on feature films as a technical survival consultant, participated in different network television programs, a frequent podcasts guest, conducts radio appearances, and speaks in front of international crowds on all topics relating to survival, bushcraft and primitive skills. Known as the "Professional Caveman" Donny is nothing, but a professional, adventurous and creative human being. Donny runs a successful wilderness self-reliance and survival school called Paleo Tracks Survival in Colorado Springs, Colorado.

Made in the USA
Coppell, TX
03 March 2021

51224599R00080